THE INDIAN ECONOMY: CRISIS, RESPONSE AND PROSPECTS

A. Vaidyanathan is currently Professor Emeritus at the Madras Institute of Development Studies. He has extensive experience in research and in policy-making institutions in India and abroad. He has been on several expert committees of the government and served briefly as a member of the Planning Commission. His research has focussed mainly on various aspects of agricultural development, employment, income distribution and the wider aspects of development strategy and planning.

TRACTS FOR THE TIMES

Editorial Board
S Gopal • Romila Thapar

Editor
Neeladri Bhattacharya

ALSO IN THE SERIES

Khaki Shorts and Saffron Flags
Tapan Basu, Pradip Datta, Sumit Sarkar, Tanika Sarkar and
Sambuddha Sen

Environmental Consciousness and Urban Planning
M N Buch

The Question of Faith
Rustom Bharucha

Kashmir: Towards Insurgency
Balraj Puri

Ayodhya: Archaeology after Demolition
D Mandal

Global Capitalism and the Indian Economy
C T Kurien

COVER: SUSETTA BOZZI

TRACTS FOR THE TIMES / 7

The Indian Economy: Crisis, Response and Prospects

A. VAIDYANATHAN

Orient Longman

THE INDIAN ECONOMY: CRISIS, RESPONSE AND PROSPECTS

Orient Longman Limited

Registered Office
3-6-272 Himayatnagar
Hyderabad 500 029 (A.P.)

Other Offices
Bombay, Calcutta, Madras, New Delhi
Bangalore, Bhubaneshwar, Cochin, Guwahati, Hyderabad, Lucknow,

© Orient Longman Ltd., 1995
First published 1995

ISBN 81-250-0316-9

Typeset by
Scribe Consultants
B4/30 Safdarjung Enclave
New Delhi 110 029

Printed in India at
SDR Printers
A28 West Jyoti Nagar, Shahdara
Delhi 110 032

Published by
Orient Longman Limited
1/24 Asaf Ali Road
New Delhi 110 002

To Shanta

Acknowledgements

The author thanks S. Neelakantan, C.T. Kurien and Asha Krishnakumar for reading and commenting on an earlier draft, and P.S. Syamala for typing the paper.

Contents

List of Tables

Editorial Preface

The New Economic Policies mark the end of an era, a sweeping reorientation of development strategy, a sharp break with the Nehruvian project of planning for development. When planning became part of the Congress economic programme in the 1930s, socialism offered a model of alternate society; and the transformation of the planned Soviet economy impressed many. Centralized planning was seen as necessary for the constitution of the nation state, for equity and development. With the crisis of socialism and the structural changes in the world, social visions and languages of discourse have been transformed. While the concepts of socialism and planning seem stale to many, the language of laissez faire which had faced a long crisis, appears to have regained legitimacy. The rhetoric of globalization and liberalization has acquired a seductive charm.

To understand the meaning of liberalization and define a perspective for the future it is necessary to move back in time, look at the history of planning, and assess the problems and contradictions of different development strategies. This tract seeks to do that—it traces the evolution of economic thinking since the 1930s, notes the major shifts within it, evaluates the performance of the economy under planning, and finally provides a nuanced critique of the liberalization programme. Vaidyanathan shows that under planning the Indian economy did develop in many ways. There was a definite break with the era of colonial backwardness, an acceleration of growth rates, an expansion of the industrial base, and a moderate increase in per capita income. But planned targets remained elusive, and the optimism of the planners dampened over the years. The GDP grew four fold since the 1950s, but population increase kept pace. So India's per capita GDP growth rate has been lower than several other Asian countries. Exports increased very slowly leading to persistent balance of payment problems. Inter-state disparities in per capita output of goods and services widened, feeding into inter-regional conflicts of interests. The public sector performance remained disappointing: gross profits in the private sector were over double that in the public sector. Unable to finance fresh investments from internal sources the public sector depended on borrowed funds. It absorbed an increasingly large portion of the total savings, instead of contributing to it. So the expansion of public investments meant fiscal imbalances.

What went wrong? In developing a critique of the planning experience, Vaidyanathan reviews a variety of arguments that seek to explain the constraints on growth. Moving beyond economic reasoning, he focuses on the political problems: the conflicts between the Centre and states, the tensions between different constituents of the ruling coalition, the structures of bureaucratic controls. Inefficient management, overmanning, waste of resources, and corruption have become an integral part of the public sector operation. But Vaidyanathan is careful to distance himself from the assumptions which underlie the recent move towards structural reforms. Problems are not inherent in the very notion of planning and State intervention, nor would all problems evaporate with liberalization.

When structural adjustments were initiated in 1991 the

Indian economy was facing a major crisis. Foreign exchange reserves had dwindled to an all-time low, India was about to default on debt repayment, its credit rating had collapsed, balance of payment deficits and budget deficits had peaked. This crisis revealed the deeper crisis which had been in the making. From 1978-79, the revenue surplus over expenditure had begun to decline. By 1984-85, current revenues fell short of current expenditures. Through the 1980s, revenue deficits rose sharply while public expenditure was expanded to stimulate growth. Increased public borrowing and monetary financing necessary to meet expenditure, enlarged the internal debt and spurred inflation. The budget measures of the reform regime sought to reduce fiscal and balance of payment deficits, cut public investments, and reduce borrowings from the Reserve Bank.

This tract looks closely at the nature of the structural adjustments and points to their limits. The reduction of fiscal deficit has been confined to the central budget; actual deficits as a percentage of GDP have been well over anticipated estimates; and this reduction has been achieved through a slash in capital account which would slow economic growth. Foreign exchange reserves have expanded but primarily due to IMF and World Bank loans, and a stagnation of imports. Industrial production and GDP are increased at a rate lower than that of the inflationary 1980s.

Vaidyanathan is emphatic about the need for reforms, but questions the ideas of present reformers. Liberalization, he argues, should not mean the end of State intervention and planning. Planning will remain important for outlining a long term view of development, reviewing overall trends of economic performance, anticipating possible new opportunities of economic expansion. Bureaucratic controls need to be relaxed, but the State cannot remain passive. It has to intervene selectively, cautiously and with greater effectivity. Import of technology can be welcomed, but its flow has to be regulated. What is necessary, according to Vaidyanathan, is a discriminatory policy of technological import backed by indigenous organizations for absorbing the techniques and adapting them. Vaidyanathan argues for the need to learn from the East Asian experience. Korea, Taiwan and Japan have all achieved their impressive rates of growth in recent decades through purposive State action, not through a policy of laissez faire.

1

Introduction

Early in 1991, before the Narasimha Rao government assumed office, India was in the midst of an unprecedented foreign exchange crisis. The country's foreign currency reserves, which had been falling for some years, dwindled precipitously in the wake of the Iraqi war. By March 1991, as a result of the sharp rise in oil prices and withdrawal of foreign currency deposits, the reserves fell to $2.2 billion (equivalent to barely one month's imports) and touched an all-time low of $1.1 billion at the end of June 1991. The country came perilously close to defaulting on interest and repayment obligation on foreign debt. India's credit rating in foreign money markets had become so low that it was practically impossible to secure short-term commercial borrowing. Also, the economy was in the grip of severe inflation and the finances of both the Centre and the states were in a poor state.

The crisis was neither sudden nor unexpected. India's balance of payments deficit with the rest of the world, the government budget deficit and the burden of external and internal public debt were progressively increasing through the 1980s. Policies which led to this deterioration had been widely criticized. The necessity for strong corrective measures to reverse these trends and restore the health of the economy had been emphasized by several observers as well as the Planning Commission in the context of the formulation of the eighth plan. That nothing was done until a payments crisis actually recurred is a commentary on the fluidity of the political situation and the weakness of the government. The crisis, however, left no option but to act.

A series of emergency measures (including the pawning of gold reserves and arranging exceptional financing) helped to tide over the immediate crisis. The World Bank, the International Monetary Fund (IMF) and the donor governments—who were approached for additional assistance to manage the balance of payments difficulties in the medium term—insisted on a credible set of policies to achieve and sustain within a reasonable period, a more viable balance of payments. This pressure unquestionably was crucial in forcing the government to put together a package of policy changes.

The 1991-92 budget indicated a number of measures to bring down the fiscal and the balance of payments deficits in the short run. The central government sought to achieve a substantial reduction in its fiscal deficit through a drastic reduction in food and fertilizer subsidies, containing the growth of non-plan expenditures and reducing the extent of budgetary resources made available to public enterprises for their plan schemes. Recourse to borrowing from the Reserve Bank was also sought to be substantially reduced. On the balance of payments front, the main measures included substantial depreciation of the rupee, containment of import growth by a severe squeeze on credit for imports and arrangements for exceptional financing to take care of the immediate debt service payments and build foreign exchange reserves.

But the situation demanded more than short-term measures. In order to achieve macro-economic stability, insure against the recurrence of such crises and at the same time promote sustained, self-reliant growth, the government has embarked on a programme of structural reform of far reaching importance. Though all the elements of the reform are yet to be worked out, the measures implemented so far, and those which are proposed, leave no doubt that it seeks the sweeping reorientation of development strategy, a narrowing of the State's role in the process and, as a corollary, major changes in the focus and means of State intervention. During the last two years many important changes have occurred in the policies relating to foreign trade and payments, taxation and government expenditures, industry and financial institutions, and the public enterprises. Many more are contemplated. The Government of India has recently published a discussion paper[1] giving a comprehensive view of the reform programme and its rationale. In order to appreciate the range and depth of the structural reform it is useful to review the main features of the programme.

FOREIGN TRADE AND INVESTMENT

In the sphere of foreign trade, practically all import control and licensing regulations have been abolished. All commodities other than consumer goods can be freely imported and the intention is to progressively remove the restrictions even on consumer goods. Import duties have been substantially reduced and the aim is to bring the rates down to an average of about 25 per cent in 1996-97 (compared to 87 per cent in 1990-91) and to simplify and rationalize the rate structure. Imports of gold and silver, which were earlier banned, are now permitted subject to payment of a small duty. The rupee has been devalued and the rate of exchange between the rupee and foreign currencies will no longer be fixed by the government but allowed to be determined by the market. Restrictions on the export of certain commodities (especially agricultural products) have been relaxed. The declared

3

intention is to phase out all quantitative restrictions on exports as quickly as possible. The policy of restricting private foreign investment has been abandoned in favour of active wooing of such investment on a much larger scale and on more liberal terms than was ever considered in the last four decades.

FISCAL POLICY

In its attempt to reduce the fiscal deficit, the central government has sought to effect large cuts in food and fertilizer subsidies, and exercise greater control over the growth of non-development expenditures, including especially defence expenditure. More important, the quantum of resources provided through the budget to finance investments of public enterprises has been reduced, and increase in the central government assistance to states (other than the mandatory transfers in accordance with recommendations of the Finance Commission) have been moderated. The decision to progressively disinvest a sizeable part of the government's equity holdings in public enterprises also signals a major shift in policy.

Over the longer run the Centre intends to intensify 'reduction and redirection' of subsidies over a wider range of goods and services (including irrigation and electricity) provided by the public sector. Restrictions on budget support to public undertakings and disinvestment of government equity in public enterprises will continue. The government also hopes to further contain the burden which the budget has to bear on account of public enterprises by closing down non-viable enterprises or selling them to the private sector, and by allowing the private sector to enter freely in areas hitherto reserved for, or dominated by, the public sector.

Simultaneously, a comprehensive reform of both direct

4

and indirect taxes aimed at simplifying the system, broadening the tax base and reducing the incentives to evasion is on the agenda. Concrete and detailed proposals for such reform have been made by two expert committees appointed specially for the purpose. A beginning has been made by lowering the maximum rate of income tax, abolishing wealth tax on 'productive assets' and introducing a scheme of presumptive taxation of small businesses to widen the tax base. In the case of excise duties, the aim is to replace the current highly differentiated and complex system (in which some commodities are taxed on the basis of physical units and others on the basis of value, and commodities are subject to tax at several points from the point of production through various stages of their transformation before they reach the final users) with a value added tax. Tariff reduction and rationalization is the third major element in the reform. A systematic reform to modernize the entire system of tax administration is also envisaged.

These changes are expected to yield significant increase in tax revenues. But more important, the rationalization of structure is expected to avoid several sources of distortion in the existing system: in particular the virtual exclusion of the unorganized sector from the scope of income and excise duties; collecting excise and sales tax at several points; and the relatively high rates of indirect taxes charged on raw material and intermediate goods compared to consumer goods. Significant changes in relative prices, costs and returns of commodities which are bound to ensue will, it is believed, promote greater efficiency all round and thus be beneficial to the economy.

DISMANTLING CONTROLS

Deregulation and getting rid of bureaucratic controls, along with liberalization of trade, technology and capital inflows are by far the most far-reaching changes in the policy regime under the reform. It was part of the original package announced in June 1991. While claiming that this has met with strong positive response and produced significant benefits in the last two years, the discussion paper recognizes that "fetters on industrial investments and production are still pervasive in the states. Requirement for licences, permits and inspections at the state and local level continue to be onerous and enterprises face difficulties in procuring land, electricity and water connections. The responsibility for necessary reform is left to the states. The penalty for not reforming will be loss of opportunities for expansion of industrial output and employment".

At the central level the main thrust of further policy changes is on "eliminating remaining barriers to industrial production, investment and import of technology" as quickly as possible and focus more on "restructuring unviable enterprises, ensuring fair business practices, safeguarding consumer interests and minimizing adverse effects of industrialization on the environment". The establishment of a Standing Committee on Public Enterprises Restructuring and Disinvestment to work out and implement enterprise-specific action for "timely detection of incipient sickness, adoption of effective rehabilitation measures and shutting down of totally unviable loss making enterprises" is commended.

Besides the creation of a National Renewal Fund to finance voluntary retirement, retraining and redeployment of workers, the need to "review and reform current legislation for employment and industrial disputes" (especially, "the requirement for prior approval by government for closure of sick units and retrenched labour") is strongly emphasized. Amendment to the Urban Land Ceiling Act is deemed essential to facilitate the use of large funds blocked in land held by many industrial units which require expensive restructuring.

FINANCIAL SECTOR

The proposed reforms in the financial sector again mark a decisive break from the past policies reflected in the 1969 bank nationalization, government control over borrowing and lending rates and on credit allocation. The new policy allows private interests to acquire a substantial part of bank equity. In order to make the loan portfolios more sound and profitable, it envisages a ban on generalized waiver of loans, introducing "speedy and effective loan recovery procedures", better targeting of "concessional lending" to the really needy and relying on incentives rather than fiat to make banks lend more to agriculture, small industry and other priority sectors.

At the same time, there is to be a phased reduction in the proportion of deposits which the banks are required by law to keep with the Reserve Bank and which they are required to invest in government securities. The banks will also gradually be freed from restrictions on interest rates charged on loans and deposits. The public and the producers will then have a wider choice of instruments. All this is expected to promote greater competition in the financial sector leading to its more efficient functioning and more efficient use of credit.

The need for well-defined standards regarding norms of prudence to be observed by financial institutions to protect the interests of depositors and investors, and also to prevent the massive frauds and other malpractices revealed by the recent scam has been emphasized. New prudential norms and more effective mechanisms of enforcement for all segments of the financial sector are said to be in process.

Exchange rate and trade policies, the dismantling of

7

controls, and fiscal management constitute the coherent and well articulated core of the reform. Criticisms that these measures are incomplete and are indifferent to the adverse consequences of the reform process for the poorer segments have led to an elaboration of the government's intentions over a wider area. Recent pronouncements refer at length to the importance of agriculture and human resource development and of measures to provide a 'safety net' to those who are likely to be affected by the reform.

AGRICULTURE

The discussion paper on economic reforms rightly states: "No strategy of economic reform and regeneration in India can succeed without substantial and broad based agricultural development. Such development is critical for raising general living standards, alleviating deep-rooted severe poverty, assuring food security, generating a buoyant market for expansion of industry and making a substantial contribution to the national export effort". It emphasizes the need to reverse the declining trend in agricultural investment in recent years and the deterioration of irrigation and other public assets due to poor maintenance. The key to this is seen to lie in containing the huge subsidies provided for water, electricity and fertilizers and in radical restructuring of public expenditure away from subsidies in favour of durable and productive investments and adequate provision for their operation and maintenance. Other measures envisaged include upgrading the quality of research and extension support, developing technologies for dryland agriculture, improving rural infrastructure and controlling land and water degradation. Export opportunities are expected to expand as a result of the new exchange rate regime and removal of controls on the export of agricultural products.

8

INFRASTRUCTURE

Unreliable power supplies, several financial shortages and operational shortcomings in power, roads, ports, telecommunications and the like are seen as major problems. In many parts of the country, according to the discussion paper, "Infrastructure services have emerged as the single most severe bottleneck to the development of agriculture, industry and exports". The policy changes to remedy this situation include induction of private sector (including foreign investment), insisting that public entities operate on commercial principles without support from the budget, diversification of ownership, and establishment of independent regulatory authorities.

THE QUESTION OF EQUITY

The discussion paper goes on at some length to meet the criticism that structural reform will hurt the poor and lists a number of measures intended to benefit the poor. Noting India's low position in terms of some basic indicators of human development, the paper points to the need to "redirect our priorities and spend much higher shares of the budget for education and health on primary education, basic health care and women and child welfare". Experience in other parts of the world points to the high returns to investment in primary education and the powerful impact of female literacy in reducing fertility rates. Therefore the large subsidies now being given on higher education and non-basic health care facilities, which in any case accrue to the better off, can be legitimately reduced in order to finance larger and better primary education and basic health care programmes.

The case for reducing subsidies on agricultural inputs is again rationalized on the ground that they mainly benefit the better-off farmers. The references to the need for better and speedier implementation of land and tenancy reforms, greater attention to providing infrastructure services to small and marginal farmers, and restoring the health of the rural credit systems are all obviously meant to allay fears that the reforms are anti-poor.

It further refers to the possibility that "The poorest segments of our society are bypassed by the virtuous cycles of growth in incomes and employment". The Jawahar Rozgar Yojana, IRDP and the public distribution system are meant to take care of this problem. But they need to be revamped to "ensure that the benefits are really targeted to the poorest and do not 'leak' to those less worthy" and create durable assets for the benefit of local people. The emphasis is not on a larger scale of outlays on these programmes but more on effective targeting and use of resources. The only new programme proposed is the National Renewal Fund to compensate workers who may get retrenched or may have to be retrained or redeployed as a result of more liberal policies on closure and rationalization.

Similarly the potential of village industries, crafts and small scale industry for generating non-farm employment is mentioned. But again it signals a significant shift of policy from "excessive regulation and protection" to promotion and "more effective systems of technical, credit and marketing support" to overcome "market imperfections", and end regulating measures and the "Inspector Raj" which goes with it.

The reforms currently under implementation cover only part of this agenda; all its various elements have not been worked out clearly and in sufficient detail. The important thing, however, is the extraordinarily wide scope of the agenda and the fact that it implies basic changes in the strategy and policies followed since Independence. It is therefore of some importance to understand the rationale of past strategies and its accomplishments and failures; the diagnosis of the reasons for the failures on which the new policies rest; and the prospects for the reforms.

2

Development Strategy under Planning

The recent policy changes and the larger agenda of reform are based on the understanding that central planning under the auspices of a strongly interventionist State has proved unsuccessful; and that replacing it by the market system with drastically reduced direct participation and regulation by the State will provide better, faster solutions to the country's social and economic problems. It is therefore appropriate to start with a brief discussion of the earlier approach, its background and its rationale.

THE RATIONALE FOR PLANNING

Well before Independence questions concerning the country's social and economic problems as well as the appropriate means to solve them were under active public debate. There was general agreement that political independence was a precondition to address these problems. But there were sharp differences on the desirability of indiscriminate adoption of the technology and life-styles of the industrialized countries in the name of "modernization" as well as on the ways to redress social and economic inequality. Jawaharlal Nehru succeeded in getting the Congress to formally accept land reform, modernization and planning as part of its programme. The implications were articulated in the reports of the National Planning Committee in the late 1930s.

This was the time when the success of socialist planning, as exemplified by the Soviet Union, was widely recognized and admired, even as the capitalist countries of the West were struggling with severe economic depression and unemployment. Active state intervention came to be generally accepted even in the US—the citadel of capitalism and private enterprise—as essential to prevent cyclical fluctuations in the economy. The experience of the Soviet Union was seen to suggest that purposive central planning under the State's leadership could transform the economy and society with astounding rapidity and in a way that promotes egalitarianism.

All this influenced Indian thinking on development so much so that even those—like the authors of the Bombay Plan or M. Visveswarayya—who were not votaries of socialism, saw the need for strong leadership and support from the government for speedy economic development. The idea of "planning for development" had thus taken root among a wide cross-section of influential opinion. The colonial government in fact made the first moves in this direction when it set up the Post-War Reconstruction Board in 1946. It was the precursor to the Planning Commission set up after Independence.

The first Five Year Plan[1] contains one of the clearest early formulations of the need for planning and of the State's role in it. Planning, it pointed out, involves "acceptance of a clearly defined set of objectives in terms of which to frame overall policies..., formulation of a strategy for promoting the realization of the ends defined..., and working out a rational solution to problems—an attempt to coordinate means and ends". Three features of this formulation are noteworthy:

13

1. It viewed planning as a means of utilizing available resources more effectively to initiate the development process.
2. It emphasized that elimination of poverty cannot be achieved *exclusively* through redistribution of existing wealth or through raising output. "Purposive intervention would be required... to channel economic activity within the existing social and economic order and so remodel the framework as to accommodate progressively the fundamental urges reflected in the demand for right to work, education and adequate income, protection of the aged, the sick and the disabled and ensuring that society's natural resources are used to subserve the common good" and do not result in concentration of wealth and power in the hands of a few.
3. It recognized that planners are not omniscient; that there are vast gaps in our knowledge of facts and that considerable amount of judgement is inevitable in making policy. The implication is that one has to keep learning from experience.

In the late forties and early fifties there was a wide measure of agreement among economists that the key to increasing productivity and achieving rising levels of real income lay in raising the rate of capital formation. "The level of production and material well-being a community can attain depends, in the main, on the stock of capital at its disposal; i.e. the amount of land per capita and productive equipment in the shape of machinery, buildings, tools and implements, factories, locomotives, engines, irrigation facilities, power installations and communication. The larger the stock of capital, the greater tends to be the productivity of labour and therefore the volume of commodities and services that can be turned out with the same effort".

Significantly, while noting the role of technical efficiency

14

of labour and its attitude to work, the plan saw the level of capital stock, which "embodies in concrete form the available technical knowledge", as being more basic. Indeed some economists of that time viewed the "take off" stage in the development process as the transition from low level of capital formation (around 5 per cent which was typical of many developing countries) to a level which approximated 10–15 per cent of gross domestic product.

ROLE OF THE STATE

At this time in the 1940s and early 1950s it was believed that the State could play a significant role both in raising the domestic rate of savings and in putting it to more productive use. Pre-industrial economies are predominantly rural and agricultural in character. They have land tenure systems in which a substantial part of the surplus over subsistence needs of cultivators and farm labourers gets appropriated by a small class of non-cultivating land owners and intermediaries (especially under the zamindari and other feudal forms of tenure) and used for non-essential consumption. Abolition of such exploitative and socially wasteful land tenure systems could release surplus for productive investment. Land reforms combined with taxation of agriculture (either directly or indirectly by influencing prices of agricultural commodities relative to that of manufactures) are means of exploiting this potential. Both require strong State intervention.

Apart from its role in maintaining law and order, defining and protecting property rights, enforcement of contracts and the like, the State has to take the primary responsibility for providing elementary education, basic health care, safe drinking water and other facilities which are in the nature of basic needs in any civilized society and which in addition have beneficial effects on the general level of productivity.

The latter effects—which are referred to as external economies—raise questions as to whether the market mechanism can secure the appropriate sharing of costs and benefits. Where externalities (beneficial or otherwise) happen to be significant, direct State intervention is necessary and justified.

Projects (e.g. road networks, major irrigation, steel plants, railways) which call for investments on a scale far beyond the capacity of individual investors and/or are in the nature of natural monopolies (e.g. public utilities) form another category where direct involvement of the State is deemed justifiable. In most cases even if the private sector is allowed to operate, the need for effective mechanisms to define and enforce standards, norms of efficiency, "fair" rate of return on investment and the like is universally accepted. All of this calls for State regulation, though not necessarily direct ownership and operation. During the early phases of Indian planning, given that indigenous industrial entrepreneurs were few in number and had relatively limited resources, the industrialists themselves favoured a large, direct role for the State in many of their activities.[2]

The government can also help development by creating conditions which induce people to save more. Low rates of savings are of course partly a reflection of low levels of income. But those who have relatively large incomes may prefer to spend on current consumption rather than save when there are relatively limited opportunities for investments that offer attractive returns. A relatively stagnant, slow growing economy implies that profitable opportunities for investment are limited. State intervention can help expand such opportunities in several ways.

Public mobilization of idle labour for creating productive assets especially roads, irrigation, land improvement, schools, rural hospitals etc. increase the potential productivity of private resources and thereby create profitable private investment opportunities. Under certain conditions,

16

increased public expenditure can enlarge the scope for profitable investment by creating additional demand for goods and services. Both these effects are likely to be considerably strengthened if there is a coordinated programme of investments for 'balanced development' ensuring that supplies of key inputs and services grow in step with the demand for them. This aspect is particularly important in the case of activities which are closely inter-related. With a coordinated programme, the risks of shortages or excesses of particular goods or services are substantially reduced. Reduced risks induce business to invest more.

Finally strong State intervention is a logical corollary of the goals of social justice and preventing concentration of power which have been explicitly incorporated among the Directive Principles of State Policy in the Constitution. Discrimination in favour of scheduled castes and tribes in the matter of government jobs and admission to educational institutions is one aspect of this. It was meant to correct the cumulative consequences of centuries of discrimination and neglect which these groups had suffered. In addition, the Directive Principles lay emphasis on:

1. securing to all citizens the right to an adequate means of livelihood;
2. ensuring that distribution of ownership and control of material resources is regulated in a manner which best serves the common good;
3. preventing the concentration of wealth and means of production; and
4. protecting children from being forced to work or being exploited on account of economic necessity.

Though these provisions lacked legal sanction, they do reflect the importance attached to 'social justice' and have shaped the scope and nature of State intervention even as they serve as a yardstick to measure the performance of the Indian State.

Altogether, as the first plan put it, whether one thinks of the problem of capital formation or of the introduction of new techniques or of the extension of social services or of the overall realignment of the productive forces and class relationships in society, one inevitably comes to the conclusion that a rapid expansion of the economic and social responsibilities of the State will alone be capable of satisfying the legitimate expectations of the people. This need not involve complete nationalization of the means of production or elimination of private agencies in agriculture or business and industry. It does however mean a progressive widening of the public sector and a reorientation of the private sector to the needs of a planned economy.

INDIAN PLANNING: SOME DISTINCTIVE FEATURES

While India adopted central planning under a strong interventionist State, its approach to planning differs in several crucial respects from that of the socialist economies. The latter, as is well known, had virtually abolished private property; all means of production were nationalized; the production and exchange activities of individual enterprises were supposed to conform to targets set by the planning authority. In India, much of the means of production have been and continue to be privately owned. Despite the significant expansion of the public sector, the private sector owns more than half the stock of capital and accounts for nearly three-fourths of the annual output. The market mechanism is active over most of the economy, even if it is imperfect and distorted.

Private property rights in India are protected by constitutional guarantees against State take-over without compensation. Except for a modest programme of land reform, and State control over some sectors like railways, coal mines and financial institutions, the State has as a matter of policy avoided nationalization of private property on any large scale. Instead it has relied on a mixture of direct and indirect controls to regulate private sector activity. Attempts to promote social justice have operated largely through fiscal policy—especially public expenditures and pricing of goods and services provided by the public sector. Moreover, the public sector plans have to be made and enforced in a federal system where constituent units have well defined functions and powers.

The responsibility for overall planning was vested with the Planning Commission. Appointed in 1950, the Commission's mandate was quite wide: the determination of the pool of resources to be devoted to development and the allocation of this pool between various uses and users; the review of all important programmes and projects before they are approved for implementation; and the monitoring and evaluation of their progress. Though formally an advisory body, it was expected that the Commission would be consulted on all major matters of development policy. And its composition was so conceived that expert professional opinion could be brought to bear on all important matters and at the same time ensure that its counsel will carry sufficient political weight in the councils of government.

Successive five year plans have sought to concretize the development strategy, programmes and priorities to realize the general vision of 'growth with social justice' within the framework of a democratic polity and mixed economy. The shape and content of successive plans show a certain evolutionary process reflecting changing ideas and perceptions on the potentials and constraints on development, the relative emphasis on different objectives, and the compulsions of political and economic exigencies at various points in time. A brief review of this evolution is necessary to review the planning experience in proper perspective.

EVOLUTION OF STRATEGY AND PRIORITIES

The First Plan (1951–1956) provided an incisive general analysis of the nature of the country's development problem and various options for mobilizing resources and achieving development with more equal distribution. There was special emphasis on the role of mass mobilization of idle rural labour and land reform. But on balance the plan rejected radical solutions (especially in respect of redistribution of existing wealth and incomes). The plan projected, rather optimistically, that savings and investment as a proportion of national income would rise from an estimated 5–6 per cent in the early 1950s to 20 per cent by 1968-69 and stabilize at that level thereafter. Aggregate income was expected to double in approximately twenty years and per capita income in twenty-seven years. Given the assumptions of the plan, the overall growth rate would have steadily increased before stabilizing at around 6.5 per cent a year from the late 1960s.

The plan examined various ways of increasing the rate of capital formation (including in particular the possibilities of using unemployed and underemployed people, as well as people engaged in activities of very low productivity, for productive capital formation). The latter, it may be recalled, was the strategy adopted by the Republic of China. The connection between this overall analysis and the concrete projects of development included in the plan was however rather weak.

The Second Plan underlined the political constraints on any radical solutions to redressing inequalities and re-emphasized rapid growth and diversification of economic activity through industrialization as essential for achieving and maintaining full employment at a rising level of productivity. It went on to define a coherent overall strategy[3] whose central elements included stepping up the rate of investment (but at a more moderate pace than envisaged in the first

20

plan) and a conscious policy of developing an indigenous heavy industry base (comprising metallurgical, chemical and machine building industries) to lay the foundation for accelerated self-reliant growth, with a leading role for the public sector. The encouragement of labour-intensive forms of producing mass consumer goods was seen to be a potentially important way of reconciling the conflict between emphasis on heavy industry (which would generate faster growth of income and employment in the long run) and the need to generate adequate jobs for the currently unemployed and underemployed in the transitional period.

The sharp deterioration in the foreign exchange position during the late 1950s (arising partly from export stagnation and partly from a liberal import policy) and the persistence of large deficits even after reimposition of import controls brought the foreign exchange constraint and the role of foreign aid into sharp focus. It was apparent that even under optimistic assumptions regarding the growth of exports and the progress of import substitution, India would need large foreign assistance for some time in order to achieve and maintain a reasonable rate of growth. The Third Plan therefore suggested a strategy—consisting of a more active export promotion effort and a planned use of aid to expand domestic production of imported goods—to see that dependence on aid is progressively reduced and eventually eliminated.

The plan took serious note of the unexpectedly high rate of population growth and incorporated a bigger family planning programme under state auspices. It also took note of the need to accelerate agricultural production. Besides increasing the allocations for agriculture and irrigation, a special programme for intensive development in selected districts with potential for quick increases in yield was launched. The Third Plan for the first time not only set out detailed, internally consistent, production and investment

21

targets for all major sectors for the five years immediately ahead, but also outlined the long-term tasks in key sectors.

Around this time the impact of development on the distribution of income, wealth and power came to be the focus of intense political debate. In the process, the dimensions and depth of mass poverty also came to be better appreciated.[4] This led to the suggestion that the "removal of abject poverty" should be the central objective of planning. This marked a significant shift from the emphasis on reducing relative disparities in income and wealth implicit in the earlier slogan of 'socialism' and 'socialist pattern of society'.

Assuring a basic minimum standard of living to every one was in fact the basis of the detailed outline of a 15-year plan for the period 1960–1975 prepared in the Planning Commission around 1964.[5] There was however no change in the basic strategy outlined in the second or the third plans— relying as it did primarily on achieving rapid overall growth with an active role for the public sector in generating the necessary surpluses and regulating the pattern of development, combined with fiscal interventions to mitigate inequalities and raise the consumption of the poor. The main difference was in arguing the case for, and the possibilities of, a "big push" and a much faster pace of overall growth (around 7 per annum) than visualized earlier or since (5 to 5.5 per cent a year).

BEGINNINGS OF CHANGE

The fifties and sixties were marked by relatively strong and stable governments under the control of the Congress both at the Centre and in the states as well as a clear commitment to, and support for, planning from the political leadership. The Planning Commission could impart a sense of vision, direction and an integrated overall perspective on the

22

desired course of the economy. This provided a framework in which investment allocations could be decided and the justification for particular projects and programmes could be evaluated. The Commission acquired prestige and began to play an important role in mediating the claims of different ministries, of the Centre vis-a-vis the states and of different states over limited development resources. It also pioneered independent evaluation of the actual working of selected schemes and their impact.

This atmosphere changed dramatically after the drought and the foreign exchange crisis of the mid-sixties. Some argued that dependence on large scale food imports and foreign aid called for a bolder plan. But this persuaded neither the political leadership nor the public. The growing tensions within the Congress made it difficult for the government to take the measures necessary to mobilize extra resources and improve the implementation. The failure of the donors to honour their commitments on the volume of aid and the poor response of exports to the devaluation aggravated the foreign exchange shortage. Planning was put on hold for nearly three years. The level of public investment suffered sharp cuts, which dampened private investment as well. In fact it took nearly a decade for the level of investment to regain the 1965-66 level!

The renewal of planning on a quinquennial basis in 1969 coincided with the intensification of the power struggle within the Congress. Hardly anything was done to put more substance to planning; instead the focus shifted to meet the strong criticism that the employment situation had worsened and that, contrary to their professed aims, the plans had not substantially reduced mass poverty or socio-economic inequalities. This is reflected in a reiteration of the 'socialist' commitment of the Congress, bank nationalization, the passing of Monopolies and Restrictive Trade Practices Act, the attempted nationalization of wholesale trade in foodgrains and later the adoption of *Garibi-hatao* and the 20-point programme.

The loosening of Congress 'hegemony', the dissensions and splits in the Congress, the emergence of non-Congress governments in several states (and eventually the Centre) during the seventies was hardly conducive, in an era of competitive electoral politics, for a rational consensus on development goals and priorities or for adopting tough measures either to mobilize more resources or for using them more effectively. The tendency on the other hand was towards placating powerful and vocal segments (typically urban consumers, agriculturists, organized sector employees) by not raising prices of goods and services provided by the public sector in step with rising costs. There was a tendency (exemplified by electricity and land revenue) to actually reduce rates and taxes. Simultaneously the poorer classes were wooed with anti-poverty programmes.

Mrs. Gandhi's success in the 1972 elections based on the *Garibi- hatao* slogan and the 20-point programme made every party adopt it thereafter. The range, variety and scale of anti-poverty programmes expanded rapidly with attempts to differentiate and package them variously to enhance their electoral appeal. A part of these programmes was meant to generate additional rural employment; some to help the poor augment their productive assets and make them more productive; while others (comprising an assortment of welfare schemes) subsidized current consumption. The growing emphasis on poverty alleviation implies that the politicians felt compelled to pay heed to the needs of the poor if only because they constitute a significant segment of the electorate. For this reason these programmes cannot be dismissed as wholly populist. But populism prevented successive governments, irrespective of party affiliation, to mobilize tax and non-tax revenues while granting indiscriminate subsidies.

The Planning Commission had by then also accepted the

defect of the 'big push-high growth' strategy and actively supported the political initiatives for expansion of anti-poverty programmes. But instead of ensuring that these programmes were properly targeted and efficiently implemented, it acquiesced in their proliferation, in the tendency to make them 'soft' by making them subsidy-intensive and failed to check the growing central control over these programmes. The role of the Planning Commission as a force in favour of greater mobilization and efficient use of resources was weakened in the process. And this tendency was reinforced following the abortive attempt at 'tough government' during the Emergency.

There was a distinct erosion in the political commitment to earlier policies. Mounting criticism led to officially sponsored reviews of the control system and public enterprise restructuring.[6] That these reviews were all done outside the aegis of the Planning Commission is perhaps symptomatic of its declining role. In the event, opinion within the leadership of the Congress began to veer to the view that the entire control system and even the roles of the public and the private sectors needed rethinking.

Despite all this, the fiscal and balance of payments situation was manageable in the seventies because of some special circumstances. This period witnessed a significant improvement of public sector performance in generating savings. Indeed public sector savings as a proportion of gross domestic product reached an all time high of 4.9 per cent in 1976-77 compared to a little over 3 per cent in the early 1960s and a little under 3 per cent in the early 1970s. The government's fiscal policy also remained conservative. Though the squeeze on public investment outlays which started in the mid-sixties gave place to an expansionary policy from the mid-1970s, the expansion in public investment was much slower than the increase in both public and total savings.

25

The foreign exchange position was exceptionally favourable largely due to remittances by non-resident Indians, especially migrant workers in West Asia whose number increased dramatically as a result of the oil boom. Total remittances rose from a mere $209 million in 1970-71 (10 per cent of receipts from exports of goods and services), to nearly $2.9 billion in 1980-81 (25 per cent of total exports). Increased domestic production of crude oil from the Bombay High oil fields (which had been discovered and explored earlier but were brought into production by investing part of the foreign assistance) was another important factor. Domestic crude oil production rose from 6.8 million tons in 1970-71 (36–67 per cent of total quantity refined) to 29 million tons (over 80 per cent of the total quantity refined) in 1984-85.

The situation changed dramatically in the 1980s, especially under the Rajiv Gandhi regime, when the government embarked on an aggressively expansionist policy without any attempt to tackle difficult problems of mobilizing revenues. The fiscal deficit grew apace and there was no hesitation in financing it through borrowing and deficit finance. At the same time the foreign exchange position deteriorated due to a slow-down in exports, the cumulative effect of large commitments on account of non-development imports during the early eighties and unrestrained commercial borrowing on hard terms. The 1991 crisis was thus predictable though perhaps its timing was hastened by the Gulf war. The political situation had become increasingly fluid. Opinion in and outside the ruling party had swung decisively in favour of liberalization and away from planning.

3

Performance under Planning

The performance of the economy is reflected in the rate at which the total output of goods and services (called the gross domestic product or GDP) has grown; the extent of diversification in the pattern of output; improvement in the living standards of the average person and also of the relatively poorer segments; and changes in the disparities of income and living standards across regions and classes. Whether or not performance has been satisfactory can of course be judged only with reference to what was expected and/or what has been achieved by other countries.

OVERALL INDICATORS

GDP Growth: During the four decades since 1950-51 the country's GDP has grown four-fold, i.e. at an average annual rate of 3.7 per cent (see Table 1). Overall growth was more or less steady (at around 3.5 per cent a year) between 1950 and 1980; growth during the 1980s (5 per cent a year) was faster. There is some reason to believe that this somewhat abrupt quickening of the pace of growth may have started even in the mid-seventies.

Since the mid-70s, all sectors have grown but at disparate

27

rates. The output of agriculture, animal husbandry, fishery, forests and mining (together referred to as the primary sector) has risen some 2.8 times in the past forty years while that of manufacturing, construction, electricity, gas etc. (collectively referred to as the secondary sector) has grown seven-fold and that of the tertiary sector (consisting of trade, transport, banking, public administration) by about six times. The share of the primary sector in the country's GDP has dropped from around 55–56 per cent in 1950 to less than a third in the late eighties; while that of the secondary sector has nearly doubled (from 14–15 per cent to 28–29 per cent) and that of services rose from approximately 30 per cent to around 40 per cent. The diversification of production is unquestionably desirable.

Capital Formation: Capital accumulation, which is an important source of growth, has risen. In the early 1950s fresh investments (including replacement of productive assets which have worn out) constituted less than 10 per cent of the country's GDP. By the late 1980s more than 22 per cent of GDP was being invested (see Table 2). One can see three distinct phases in the behaviour of investment. The first, lasting approximately the first fifteen years of planning, saw a more or less sustained increase. Then followed a period of relatively stable investment rate but at levels lower than those reached around 1964-65. This phase lasted nearly a decade before giving place to a phase of renewed increase in investment.

Upto the end of the 1970s, the growth of GDP was not commensurate with the expansion of investment. In other words the additional investment needed to generate an extra unit of output (called the Incremental Capital Output Ratio or ICOR) had risen substantially. Though this trend has been reversed in the eighties, the ICOR is still higher than in the 1950s. This is widely interpreted as a sign of the low level of efficiency with which investment is utilized.

28

Financing of Capital Formation: In the early 1950s investments were almost wholly financed by internal savings. Thereafter the proportion of investment financed by foreign aid and borrowing rose progressively till the latter half of the sixties when foreign resources accounted for nearly one-fourth of the total investments. The position was reversed dramatically during the seventies, partly because of a significant rise in domestic savings and partly due to the moderate increase of investments. During the late seventies the country's savings were adequate (in some years more than adequate) to finance the investments undertaken within the country. This trend was reversed in the eighties reflecting a tendency for investments to grow faster than domestic savings (see Table 2).

Foreign aid and capital inflows represent the difference between the payments made abroad (for import of goods and services, repatriation of profits earned on accumulated foreign investments in India, and interest and repayment of principal on account of accumulated debts, official and private) and the receipts of foreign exchange (on account of export of goods and services, gifts and remittances from abroad, and interest, dividend etc. on Indian investments abroad). The increased dependence on aid in the late fifties and the sixties basically reflects the relatively slow growth of exports compared to imports despite strict control over imports during most of this period. The reduced dependence on aid in the seventies reflects in part the strong performance of exports but more importantly the phenomenal increase in remittances from migrant Indian workers in West Asia and elsewhere (see Table 3). The deterioration of the eighties was due to several reasons: relatively slow export growth; slowing down in the growth of remittances; and recourse to large scale commercial borrowing at high interest rates.

Agriculture: Agricultural production as a whole has grown more or less at a constant rate (2.6 per cent a year)

29

throughout. During the early 1950s the major part of the additional production came from expansion in cultivated areas and more intensive cropping of land. Gradually the scope for bringing new land under the plough has been exhausted. While land already under cultivation is being used more and more intensively (by growing a second or even a third crop in a given year) the bulk of the increase in output now comes from higher production per acre of cropped area. The rate of yield improvement (taking all crops together) has steadily increased and is currently about twice the rate realized in the fifties.

The higher rate of yield improvement since the 1950s, and their quickening pace, is the result of an active programme of public investment and a price policy which supported agriculture. Total irrigated area rose from nearly 23 million ha in 1950-51 to 60 million ha in 1989-90. The proportion of irrigated areas served exclusively by ground water—which is superior to canals and tanks in providing dependable and timely water supply—has risen from 29 per cent to over 50 per cent. Use of ground water in conjunction with surface water which again makes for better quality irrigation has also grown. The research network of the Indian Council of Agriculture Research has evolved improved crop varieties—high yielding varieties of cereals being the most dramatic example—and agricultural practices which the National Extension Services have propagated among farmers. Fertilizer use, which was negligible in volume and restricted to a few regions and crops, is now very widely diffused. The total quantity used (in terms of plant nutrients) now exceeds 13 million tonnes a year (see Table 4). There has been a vast expansion in rural transport network, in the marketing and distribution system and in institutional credit facilities. The government's price support policy and subsidized supply of inputs have also played a role in facilitating agricultural growth.

30

However, there are wide differences in the growth of different crops and regions. Wheat has recorded the fastest rate of growth; paddy, sugarcane and cotton have also experienced sustained growth though not as fast as wheat. However, crops like millet, pulses and groundnut have done poorly. In general, much if not most of the increase in production has come from irrigated land, whose extent has grown as have yields per hectare. The performance of rainfed agriculture is poor. There is in fact reason to believe that overall productivity of unirrigated land has grown little, if at all.

Vast regional differences in growth are another characteristic of agricultural performance. According to one recent estimate the rate of output growth between the early sixties and early eighties ranged from less than 1 per cent per year (in Tamil Nadu and Bihar) to over 6 per cent a year (in Punjab). The variations at the district level are even more dramatic. Over the same period 17 out of 281 districts for which estimates have been made experienced an absolute decline in output; 82 had growth rates below 1.5 per cent a year while, at the other extreme, 23 districts posted rates better than 5 per cent a year.

Industry: The contribution of manufacturing to the country's GDP has risen six-fold between 1951–55 and 1986–90. The first three plans witnessed relatively faster growth than during the late sixties and the seventies. The eighties witnessed a significant revival of industrial growth till the crisis of 1991. The last two years have shown hardly any growth in industry.

The structure of manufacturing has undergone major changes. First, factory type industry—which consists of relatively large, modern manufacturing establishments using power and machinery—has grown much faster than small scale and cottage units falling outside the Factories Act. The factory sector's share in manufacturing output has risen from around 46 per cent in 1951–55 to 59 per cent in 1985–90. Second, within the small-cottage sector, household-type industries making traditional products with traditional techniques (like handlooms, processing of agricultural produce, pottery and the like) have declined sharply, especially in rural areas. On the other hand modern small industry—relatively better organized units producing newer types of products and services (mostly repairs) and employing more modern techniques—has grown rapidly both in rural and urban areas. There is reason to believe that employment in this modern small scale sector (which includes powerlooms, garment-making, engineering and electronics units) has grown at a rapid rate. Its share in total manufacturing output and employment has increased sharply.

The third aspect is the diversification of the industrial base. At the time of Independence modern industry consisted largely of cotton and jute textiles; metals, cement and engineering industries were in a nascent stage. Today manufacturing capability is incomparably wider and deeper producing not only a large range of consumer goods (including items like automobiles, consumer electronics, refrigerators and washing machines) but also practically all important industrial raw materials (metals, metal alloys, fertilizers, petrochemicals, refineries etc.) and a wide range of electrical and non-electrical machinery and transport equipment (see Table 5). This diversification has occurred both in large and small industry sectors but is considerably more striking in the factory sector. In the first plan period, about 65 per cent of output was from consumer goods, about one-fourth was contributed by intermediate goods (raw and semi finished materials) and barely 10 per cent by capital goods. Today (late 1980s) the three categories contribute more or less equally to the factory sector's output.

The growth of the indigenous industrial entrepreneurial

class and the emergence of several new centres of manufacturing industry are the other notable characteristics of development during the last four decades. Under colonial rule, foreign enterprises were dominant in the country's modern industrial sector: they controlled and managed much of jute industry, and a good part of cotton textiles, cement, paper and chemicals. Since Independence, the government has restricted the entry of foreign private capital. Gradually several of the pre-existing foreign enterprises have been acquired by indigenous business. Though new foreign collaborations are widespread, the extent of direct participation in ownership and management by foreign firms has so far been quite limited.

Some of the present large Indian business houses (notably the Tatas, Birlas, Dalmias and the leading mill owners of Bombay and Ahmedabad) had established modern industry in the pre-Independence period. Even as they have grown and diversified their activities since—and some have grown very rapidly indeed—a large number of new houses have emerged all over the country. The top twenty big business houses controlled about 39 per cent of the net assets of the private corporate sector in 1958-59. The majority of houses which were in this list do not figure among the top twenty in 1989-90. Several new houses have emerged, some of them (like the Ambanis) recording phenomenal growth. The share of the largest twenty houses in the net assets of the private corporate sector in 1989- 90 (25 per cent) is also considerably lower than in the late 1950s.[1]

In the early fifties modern industry was mostly concentrated in and around Bombay, Calcutta and Madras. Ahmedabad, Coimbatore and Kanpur were the main interior centres with any significant industrial activity. Dispersal of industry has been one of the objectives of policy under planning. While this has not prevented the continued growth of the older industrial centres—in fact a sizeable part of industrial

' activity is still concentrated in and around them—the importance of cities like Ahmedabad, Bangalore, Hyderabad, Coimbatore, Baroda has grown. Several new centres like Bhopal, Bhilai, Bokaro, and Ludhiana have come into prominence.

Living Standards: Ultimately a larger and more varied output of goods and services is meant to provide a better life to people. The level of real income per head of population is used as a rough overall measure of well-being. On this criterion, there has been some improvement over the last four decades with per capita income at constant prices recording a near doubling between 1950-51 and 1990-91. But per capita income alone is now widely recognized as an inadequate measure of living standards. One should look at the improvement in the availability, on the average, of basic goods like food, clothing and shelter, the state of health, levels of literacy and the like, as well as the proportion of the population who can afford a specified minimum standard of consumption of such basic items (see Table 6).

The per capita availability of foodgrains for the country as a whole in the late 1980s was about 13 per cent higher than in early 1950s, but barely 3 per cent higher than in the early 1960s. The per capita availability of fat has risen by 70 per cent; that of cloth (adjusting for difference in quality of cotton and man-made fabrics) by 60 per cent; tea by 84 per cent and white sugar has more than doubled. Enrolment in elementary schools as a proportion of children in the age group 5–14 has risen from 25 per cent to 50 per cent; and overall literacy rate from 18 per cent to 52 per cent. Death rates, both overall and among infants, have fallen and the expectation of life at birth has increased from 32 to 60 years. The expansion of roads and railways makes people more mobile even as exposure to mass media (especially cinema, radio and television) vastly increases peoples' awareness of what is happening outside their immediate environment and of the possibilities opened up by modern industry.

DEFICIENCIES AND FAILURES

Overall Growth: In terms of growth, increasing the rate of investment, diversification of the economy and the building of a broad industrial base, the achievements in the post-Independence period are unquestionably impressive when contrasted to the near stagnation of the economy in the first half of the century.[2] However, viewed in relation to the targets set by the plans and the performance of many other developing countries, the record is not impressive.

The overall rate of growth has consistently fallen short of plan targets. The first Five Year Plan envisaged doubling per capita real income in about 25 years; but it has taken more than 40 years to reach this target. India's per capita GDP growth rate (1.8 per cent a year) is much lower than in several other Asian countries including Pakistan (2.5 per cent), Indonesia (4.4 per cent), Thailand (4.2 per cent), Republic of Korea (7 per cent) and China (5.1 per cent). India also seems to be using much more capital per unit of additional output than many of the fast growing economies of Asia. That the total value of output of manufactures in a small country like S. Korea which was one-fourth that of India in 1970 ($1.9 billion against $7.9 billion) has surpassed India's by 25 per cent in 1988 ($54 billion against $44 billion), testifies to the relatively slow pace of Indian industrialization.

Export Performance: We have already referred to the fact that despite a regime of tight restrictions on imports, India's export growth has been on the whole too slow and erratic to maintain a viable balance of payments. Indian exports have grown much slower than world export trade resulting in a substantial fall in its share in world trade (from 2 per cent at Independence to 0.5 per cent in 1990). While there has been considerable diversification of trade from tea, jute, cotton and other primary products to manufactures, the growth of manufactured exports compares very unfavourably (in volume as well as in range and sophistication) with countries like Korea, Thailand, Taiwan, Hong Kong and Singapore. Indian industry has not shown the dynamism, innovativeness and capacity to compete in world markets which these countries have. The fact that a small country like Korea exports five times as much of manufactures ($43 billion in 1989) to developed countries as India ($8 billion) dramatizes the difference in performance.[3]

Persistence of Mass Poverty: A combination of slow growth in output and relatively rapid population increase has meant that the pace of improvement in Indian living standards has also been modest. That there has been only a marginal improvement in per capita foodgrain availability suggests that improvement in nutritional status cannot be significant. A substantial proportion of the population still does not get the level of calories recommended by nutrionists. The constitutional directive of universal compulsory elementary education has still not been reached. Infant mortality rates and other indicators of health status remain at unsatisfactory levels. Per capita calorie intake, infant mortality, and literacy rates in India compare unfavourably with those obtaining in several other Asian countries; and the pace of improvement in some respects slower.

The slow pace of improvement in average living standards reflects not only the slow growth of GDP but also a high rate of population growth—currently 2.2 per cent per annum. India was one of the first developing countries to recognize the importance of birth control and has been implementing a sizeable family planning programme for over three decades. The results however have been disappointingly meagre. The crude birth rate has of course declined from around 40 per 1000 in 1950-51 to about 30 per 1000 in 1990-91. Over the same period death rates have declined much faster (from 27 per 1000 to 10 per 1000). Consequently the net rate of population growth actually rose for a while, from around 1.6 per cent per annum in the early 1950s to 2.2 per cent in the early 1970s. There has been a decline since, but only a moderate decline. By the end of the 1980s population was still growing by close to 2 per cent a year. The relatively modest achievements of family planning are attributed to several factors including the very low levels of female literacy (even in 1990 half the Indian women were illiterate!) and inadequacies in terms of resources devoted to family planning, as well as in the conception, organization and management of the whole programme.

Employment Trends: There is widespread belief that slow growth combined with policies encouraging techniques of production which are more capital and less labour-intensive have resulted in increasing unemployment and under-employment. It is also believed that inequalities in the distribution of income and wealth have worsened; the evidence is mixed. Prima facie there are good reasons to apprehend that the employment situation may have worsened: the population and labour force have been growing rapidly; land holdings are getting smaller because of the growing pressure of population on available land; tenants are being evicted and an increasing proportion of the rural labour force is becoming dependent on wage labour; opportunities for employment in agriculture have not really grown partly because output growth relative to population is low and partly because techniques which displace labour (tractors, combine harvestors, threshing machines) have spread fast.

Under these circumstances there is good reason to expect

growing unemployment and under-employment and a downward pressure on wages in rural areas and in the unorganized segment of the urban areas. This would tend to depress the real incomes of the wage labourers especially when they are not organized into effective trade unions. A small segment of the non-agricultural work force belongs to the latter class (mostly concentrated in factory industry, large trading establishments, financial institutions and the public sector) and their real incomes have in fact risen appreciably. One would expect all this to result in a worsening of the disparities in income distribution between propertied classes and labourers, between workers in the organized sector and those employed in unorganized sectors and between rural and urban areas.

Evidence from carefully designed surveys of the National Sample Survey Organization (NSSO), however, *do not* indicate an all-round deterioration on the employment front. It is certainly true that the proportion of workers depending on work for wages is increasing and that agricultural employment is increasing, if at all, very slowly. However, the open unemployment rate is not rising everywhere or consistently. On the other hand data suggests that there is a substantial rise in total employment in both rural and urban areas and the bulk of this is in a wide range of non-agricultural activities (see Table 7). Real wage rates have not fallen; if anything there may be some rise at least during the seventies and eighties.

Trends in Income Distribution: Official estimates do suggest that the inter-state disparities in per capita output of goods and services (measured by the State Domestic Product), the density of road network and the number of hospital beds per' capita have widened. There has, however, been some reduction in inter-state disparities in respect of per capita electricity consumption, factory employment and literacy rates. The

38

differential between the income generated per worker in agricultural and non-agricultural activities has increased. The earnings of organized sector workers have risen considerably faster than the average implying a widening differential between organized and unorganized sectors.

As for checking the concentration of industry and finance in the hands of a few big business houses, some studies in the 1960s showed that despite the licensing system, big business houses continued to grow and that their share in total assets of the corporate sector had not declined. There are no studies of the impact of the subsequent nationalization of banks and of the Monopolies and Restrictive Trade Practices Act on industrial concentration. What we do know is that a number of new large business houses have emerged, that several of the older ones have been going through a process of splitting.

Evidence from consumer surveys does not point to any tendency for the distribution of consumption (after adjusting for price changes) to become more unequal.[4] What they do show—and this is puzzling—is that even the poorest classes whose incomes have grown only modestly, seem to be switching to more expensive cereals (rice and wheat) from coarse grains; to protective food (milk, meat etc.) from cereals, and to non-food items from food. On the other hand the disparities in per capita output across states, and in the case of agricultural output across districts, have progressively increased.

There are far too many problems concerning the comparability and the reliability of some of this data for judging changes (especially, as with consumption, when changes are relatively slow). One important reason is the existence of 'black money' and the probable under-reporting of both production and consumption. The black economy has grown. While it is impossible, given its clandestine nature, to estimate its true dimensions, or the rate at which it has grown, there is no doubt that it is large. Some of the 'guesstimates' of its magnitude are truly staggering. According to one estimate Indian citizens have accumulated assets (including financial assets) amounting to $50–100 billion (Rs 150,000 to 300,000 crores). Another recent estimate places the income generated in the black economy in 1980-81 at 20 per cent of official estimate of national income in that year.[5]

Black money is generated in various ways: the more important among them being illegal distillation and sale of alcohol, kickbacks on public sector purchases and contracts, concealment of incomes and production to evade taxes, bribes for appointments, promotions and transfers in public services, bribes to avoid compliance with the law or to avoid penalties for violating them, over-invoicing of imports and under-invoicing of exports, and smuggling of commodities, gold and drugs across the national border.

Critics maintain that planning based on a large public sector, a highly regulated private sector and direct controls on foreign exchange transactions is directly responsible for the emergence of black economy. Banning the import of gold or consumer goods and restricting of others through licensing without taking effective steps to reduce the demand for these commodities creates highly profitable opportunities for smuggling. High import duties make smuggling potentially even more profitable. High tax rates induce evasion and if tax officials are amenable, the evaders stand to reap large gains. This has no doubt happened and is still happening. That kickbacks on public sector purchases and contracts are widespread is common knowledge; so is the corruption associated with the enforcement of the numerous regulations on the private sector. The softness of the administration in enforcing laws and the corruption related to appointments, promotions and transfers in public sector employment can hardly be attributed to planning.

If the black economy has been growing faster than the

'white' economy, it is because the former is largely concentrated among the well-to-do. The various surveys not only understate the extent of inequality in society but also the extent to which the disparities in the distribution of income and wealth have grown.

The fact remains that even by the very modest minimum standards set by the Planning Commission, and the distribution as revealed by official surveys, about 40 per cent of rural India (250 million people!) are still poor. Roughly 66 per cent of the rural and 57 per cent of the urban population do not have even 2250 kilocalories per head per day.[6] Around 60 per cent of the people belonging to the poorest twenty per cent of the population are illiterate; elementary school enrolment rate in this class is still less than 75 per cent, and the incidence of mortality remains high. Poverty remains a massive problem.

Public Savings: One of the central premises of the plans from the beginning has been that the government and its enterprises would make a major contribution to raising the overall rate of savings. It was expected that public savings would form an increasing proportion of total savings and that a large part of public investment would be financed by its own savings. None of these expectations have been realized. Realized public savings have fallen consistently short of targets. In the first plan period total public savings averaged 1.6 per cent of GDP and the overall savings rate around 9.2 per cent. Somewhat over a half of the public sector's investment was financed by its own savings. Currently (average of 1989-90 to 1991-92), public savings are around 1.5 per cent of GDP accounting for barely 6 to 7 per cent of total savings; 85 per cent of public investment is now financed by borrowing (see Table 2).

The current situation reflects a progressive deterioration since the late 1970s. Earlier, the public savings rate had recorded a rising trend from 1950 through the mid-sixties (reaching 3.3 per cent of GDP in 1964-65); it fell and remained at a lower level for several years thereafter before reviving an upward trend. The mid-seventies saw a sizeable rise in public savings (average around 4.5 per cent) and reached an all time high of 4.9 per cent in 1976-77. But after 1978-79 there has been a steady decline and by 1990-91, the rate had fallen to 1.1 per cent of GDP. This is almost entirely due to a deterioration in the budgetary position of the Centre and the states. Savings of public enterprises as a proportion of GDP has not shown any significant trend.

The excess of government (tax and non-tax) revenue over its total current expenditure gives a measure of the savings through the budget available for financing capital formation (see Table 8). Although it was consistently below target, the rate was at least rising through the 1970s (from 1.3–1.4 per cent of GDP in the early 1970s to 2.5 per cent in the late 1970s). But from 1978-79, the revenue surplus began to decline and by 1984-85, the current revenue of the Centre and the states taken together fell short of even current expenditures . This process started somewhat earlier in the states than at the Centre. Both experienced a steep rise in the revenue deficit through the 1980s. This means that the government has had to borrow to meet part of its regular expenditure.

This deterioration is the result of several factors. First, the government has not ensured that revenues increase commensurately with expenditure especially during the eighties: upto the mid-seventies revenues rose progressively at a rate somewhat higher than revenue expenditures leading to a rising revenue surplus. The trend was reversed thereafter: while revenues continued to rise both in absolute terms and as a proportion of GDP, expenditures rose even faster.

Second, the relatively rapid increase in revenue expenditures from the latter half of the seventies was due to increase in salaries, higher interest payments and rising subsidies. The acceptance of the recommendations of the Fourth Pay Commission meant a substantial increase in the emoluments of central government employees. This led to an intensified and successful agitation by employees of state governments for parity with central scales. Since in all cases revisions were granted with retrospective effect, large payments had to be made to clear arrears due. The increase in emoluments also meant a continuing burden on the budgets of both the Centre and the states. It must be noted that the increase in emoluments per employee has been substantially more than the rate of 'inflation' and has meant a significant rise in real earnings.

The growth of subsidies has been particularly rapid: both the central and the state governments have been reluctant to raise the sale prices of goods and services supplied by them (e.g. essential commodities distributed through fair price shops, fertilizers, electricity, irrigation, public transport, co-operative credit) even though the costs of producing and distributing these commodities continued to rise. This tendency was particularly marked since the late 1970s and probably reflects the growing fluidity of politics and intensified competition among political parties. Increasing subsidies on food and fertilizers in the name of keeping prices in check for vulnerable groups was politically attractive and made a significant difference to electoral outcome. Increased export subsidies were meant to stimulate exports.

Some of these subsidies (those on food, fertilizers and exports) are made explicit in the budget but several are concealed in the inability of the departments/enterprises supplying these goods and services to earn surpluses to cover at least the interest charges on the capital converted. More often it is reflected in losses. The magnitude involved has also grown at an alarming rate. According to one estimate the magnitude of unrecovered costs on account of economic and social services provided by the states alone rose from

Rs 52 billion in 1977-78 to Rs 256 billion in 1987-88. Total unrecovered costs in 1987-88 (of Centre and states) amounted to some Rs 420 billion which is considerably higher than the total public sector plan outlay in that year (Rs 350 billion).[7] Most governments, irrespective of their party affiliation, have found it politically expedient not to insist on fuller cost recovery (whether by raising rates or by cutting costs) in respect of the above mentioned items used by large numbers of people that no party wants to alienate.

The fact that revenue expenditures and deficits of enterprises were growing faster than revenue did not deter the government from increasing expenditure on plan projects. At the time of plan formulation, the Centre and the states are all in favour of larger plans and larger sector plans. In assessing the resources available for the plan, everyone makes unrealistic assumptions that non-plan expenditure will not be allowed to grow much and undertake to mobilize the additional resources necessary to meet any gap. These tendencies, always there, have become much more acute in the last decade or so. The balance from current revenues, without taking into account projected additional mobilization, has invariably been below target. So has additional mobilization (except during the latter half of the 1970s).

Although public savings have invariably been less than projected by the plans, actual plan outlays have turned out to be higher than approved: by around 13 per cent during the sixth plan period (1980–85) and by 23 per cent in the seventh plan (1985–90). The dependence on borrowing therefore turned to be much higher and has risen much faster than projected. This and the fact that interest rates on government securities were raised steeply resulted in an extraordinary increase in both public debt and the magnitude of interest payments by the government.

Public Sector Performance: The other major criticism relates to

44

the performance of the public sector. The public sector's importance in the economy has grown enormously since Independence (see Table 9). In 1950-51 an estimated 18 per cent of the country's productive assets were in the public sector; this proportion is currently about 45 per cent. In 1950- 51 the public sector contributed about 7.5 per cent of the country's GDP; in 1990-91 its contribution rose to 26 per cent. Its share in total national expenditure which was 8.5 per cent in 1950-51 is currently 26 per cent. The public sector is solely responsible for much of the essential economic infrastructure (electricity, rail transport, road networks, ports) and has a major role in respect of some of the key inputs which enter the production process (energy, metals, fertilizers, petro-chemicals and certain categories of heavy machinery).

The main indictments against the public sector are that despite large outlays, the economy is plagued by inadequate, unreliable and high-cost infrastructure services. Inordinate delays in commissioning projects, the politicization of investment decisions and the management of public services has led to widespread corruption both in setting up and operating enterprises, lack of credible mechanisms to make the enterprises accountable to their customers and the public; and as a result, returns to investment in these enterprises are very low.

The investment used by the public sector per rupee they contribute to the GDP is much higher than the average. This is at least partly explainable by the fact that the public sector involvement is concentrated in activities which by their nature require much larger investments per unit of output than average. The more serious problem however is low returns in terms of profits earned relative to investment.

During the 1980s the gross profits of public enterprises under the control of the central government (excluding oil) averaged around 3.4 per cent of the capital employed compared to 8.8 per cent in the case of the private corporate sector. After allowing for depreciation and interest payments, they had carried a net loss accounting to a little over 3 per cent of net worth (i.e. total employed *less* borrowed capital). By comparison the private sector companies earned 12.7 per cent on net worth before taxes.[8] Thus, the profits of these enterprises were insufficient to meet even the interest obligations on borrowed capital (not to speak of giving any return on their own funds). The position of public enterprises under the state governments (mainly electricity boards, irrigation and public road transport corporations) is even worse.

The record of public enterprises taken as a whole in generating surplus has been consistently poor and consistently below the targets set in every five year plan. Thus, instead of relying more and more on internal resources (depreciation and net retained profits) to finance fresh investments as visualized by the plans, the dependence of the public sector on borrowed funds has increased. With interest rates having risen sharply, this has contributed to further aggravation of fiscal imbalance.

4

Understanding Performance

The relatively modest growth performance of the Indian economy, its relative inefficiency and its lack of technological dynamism are generally attributed to defects in the basic development strategy. The following elements are usually singled out in this connection: the heavy industry bias of the plans imparted by Mahalanobis; the neglect of agriculture and labour intensive forms of export production; a tariff-exchange-rate policy which made production for the domestic market more profitable than production for exports, and also insulated domestic industry from competitive pressures; and the excessive reliance on an inefficient public sector. These tendencies, it is argued, have been reinforced by the control system, which gave little flexibility to producers in their choice of location, scale, technology and product mix and which actively discouraged exploitation of scale economies in the name of equity.[1]

DEFECTIVE INVESTMENT STRATEGY

The criticism that poor growth is due to our planning strategy being biased in favour of heavy industry while neglecting agriculture is questionable. The heavy industry

47

orientation was strong only in the second and third plans but not thereafter. If anything, the share of public investment going to industry as a whole, and to metallurgical and machinery industries in particular, fell after the mid-sixties (see Table 10). In any case at no time was the State in a position to force the private sector to take to heavy industry. The recession in demand for these industries caused by the deceleration in public investment affected the private sector's willingness to make any fresh investment in these sectors.

Similarly, the failure to accelerate agricultural growth can hardly be explained by inadequacy of investment. Much of the investment is in spreading irrigation, improving soil and water management and in research and extension. While these are important, there is no simple or direct relation between investment and growth in output. The vast disparities in growth as between irrigated and rain-fed land, as well as across regions and crops, cannot be explained by differences in investment. They reflect uneven progress in evolving better seed varieties suited to irrigated and rain-fed conditions and for different regions and crops. Moreover there is abundant evidence that actual yield in most cases is a fraction of the yields demonstrated to be feasible with available technology. There are also indications that the incremental output per unit of input may actually be declining at a time when better varieties and the rapid spread of groundwater-based irrigation should have raised the yield response to inputs. This is in large part a reflection of the poor quality of land and water management.

The uneven success in breeding crop varieties, deficiencies in adaptive research, deficiencies in water management or for that matter soil conservation of rain-fed lands cannot be attributed to inadequate investments. The quality of design and execution of these programmes, and the institutional arrangements for proper maintenance and efficient management of facilities which serve large numbers of farmers have an important bearing on the attainable yields. This is not to suggest that the recent declining trend in agricultural investments is of no consequence but only to emphasize the role of other factors and in particular the efficacy of the organizations which make and manage the programmes.

FOREIGN TRADE POLICIES

One criticism which in retrospect has considerable validity relates to foreign exchange and trade policies. The Indian plans were certainly not based on assumptions of autarky. There was of course a strong sense of pessimism about export prospects. This pessimism was understandable in the fifties, in as much as Indian exports were dominated by primary commodities. The demand for these commodities was not growing fast and was threatened by the emergence of substitutes. Non-traditional exports also did not seem promising because of the narrow industrial base. But the extent to which the latter limitation could be overcome by appropriate policies was clearly underestimated.

The persistence with a fixed and over-valued exchange rate for the rupee and the fact that a combination of high tariffs and quantitative restrictions loaded the dice heavily in favour of import substitution and production for the domestic market worked to the disadvantage of exports. They undoubtedly created an environment in which there was hardly any incentive to scout export markets. However, the over-valued exchange rate is only part of the story. After all, despite the 1966 devaluation, the progressive and substantial depreciation of the rupee since the early 1970s and a variety of export incentives, overall export growth has been slow and erratic. The impact of devaluation on exports might have been greater if there were no restrictions on capacity/product mix and on imports of inputs, machinery and technology; and if imported inputs had not carried such high rates of duty. It has also been suggested that hesitations about tie-ups with large foreign manufacturers and trading houses may have contributed in some degree to the slow growth of exports.

We must also note that official figures do not give a complete and accurate picture of the country's foreign exchange transactions. High import duties, the ban on the import of consumer goods and precious metals which were in great demand, and the desire of businessmen and other well-to-do sections to shift part of their wealth abroad—all contributed to the emergence of smuggling and illegal transactions in foreign exchange. Exports tended to be under-invoiced so that the value of export earnings reported and surrendered to the Reserve Bank of India was less than the true realization. On the other hand imports—all of which were under licence—tended to be over-invoiced so that actual payments were more than the true value of purchases. The difference, along with the proceeds of smuggling of silver and lately, drugs, was used to finance smuggled imports of gold, commodities and for the accumulation of assets abroad. There is no way of knowing how these illegal transactions have grown. According to one estimate the exchange inflow through illegal channels in 1989-90 was $5 billion, roughly one-fourth of the total receipts on account of exports (including invisibles and remittances) through official channels.

OVER-EMPHASIS ON REDISTRIBUTION

Another criticism relates to the effect of State interventions in the name of distributive justice. According to one view— associated with the left parties—a more egalitarian distribution of wealth and incomes is an essential precondition for rapid growth catering to the essential consumption needs of the mass of the people and of course a precondition for real democracy. The failure of land reform, the failure to reduce the inequalities of wealth in private hands—at any rate the failure to bring its use under effective social control—are therefore seen as root causes of the failure of Indian planning.

An egalitarian distribution of income has obvious ethical appeal, especially in a context where a large mass of people live in abject poverty. At the same time it is uncertain if rates of saving as high as those achieved would have been feasible at the current low levels of living with an egalitarian income distribution. Also a more equal distribution does not affect aggregate demand for consumption so much as its pattern. With a more equal distribution of income, the pattern would shift in favour of food as against non-food items and a smaller quantum as well as a less diversified pattern of demand for manufactures. This would then call for a much faster growth in agriculture and a slower growth of manufactures. Whether a more equal distribution of land per se would have generated faster growth of agricultural production is also debatable.

A contrary and currently more fashionable view attributes inefficiency and slow growth to the intervention of the State to redress inequality in wealth and incomes. For instance, the restrictions on the expansion of big business houses is seen to have impeded the exploitation of scale economies. Ceilings on land and high rate of direct taxation are seen to have reduced incentives for increased production and accumulation. The various measures to protect household and small-scale industry in the name of promoting employment, besides being expensive in terms of subsidies, have meant perpetuation of high cost, low quality production in a wide range of industries. These interventions

51

together with the operation of the control system, it is suggested, may have actually aggravated inequalities in the system.

Radical land redistribution has played an important role in China, Japan and Korea in breaking up the landlord and rentier classes who used to wield immense power and stood in the way of the emergence and growth of modern capitalist entrepreneurs. It fundamentally altered the balance of political forces in favour of the latter; it also enabled the State to appropriate more of the agricultural surplus through taxes and by manipulating the prices of agricultural commodities relative to that of manufactures. But there is some question whether this is at all feasible in the Indian context and even if it were, whether land re-distribution would by itself make agriculture grow faster.[2]

Faster agricultural growth requires more investment, a large part of which has necessarily to be made by the State in infrastructure (including research, extension, rural roads and markets). It is contingent on successful research to develop superior seed varieties and agronomic practices adapted to varied local conditions. And, above all, in an agrarian system dominated by a very large number of peasants with small holdings, it is contingent on effective institutional arrangements to regulate the use of land, water and other common resources in the interests of sustaining a high level of productivity.

But all this is of no more than theoretical interest since very little has actually been done to implement even mildly redistributive measures on the statute book. By far the most important among these are the abolition of zamindari and other feudal forms of land tenure, the imposition of ceilings on land ownership, and protection of tenants and land ceilings. The first was relatively successful but its implementation was delayed by years of litigation. And there were enough loopholes in the law to permit many zamindars to retain large amounts of land for 'self cultivation'. Tenancy reforms seem to have been moderately successful in a few states, notably Kerala, Karnataka and West Bengal, where political conditions were favourable. Even in these states while the numbers benefited were large, the amount of land transferred relative to the total cultivated area has been small. Moreover, not all the benefits have accrued to marginal and small farmers. Consequently, it has made only a small difference to the inequality in the distribution of land ownership. The land ceiling legislations are widely recognized to be a near-total failure everywhere in the country.

Progressive taxation of income, wealth and inheritance have hardly reduced inequality. The level of income/wealth at which these taxes begin to operate is so high in relation to the average income per earner that only a small fraction are liable to pay. And only a fraction of those liable do in fact pay. Numerous concessions and exemptions have made administration complex and avoidance relatively easy. Instead of simplifying the tax laws and enforcing compliance more strictly, the tendency has been to reduce the tax rates on the ground that lower tax rates reduce the incentive for evasion. Inheritance taxes have been abolished.

Public expenditures—especially on elementary education, basic health care, various poverty alleviation programmes and possibly food subsidies—are *prima facie* more effective in augmenting the real incomes of the poor. But in so far as the benefits of these programmes are not confined to the poor and that those who benefit do not get the full amount due to them, their distributive impact is weakened. There is ample evidence to suggest that a substantial part of the beneficiaries of these programmes are 'non-poor' and that a sizeable part of the resources are appropriated by various intermediaries and those responsible for implementation.[3]

RESTRICTIONS ON THE PRIVATE SECTOR

The argument that Indian planning failed because it was dominated by the public sector and gave insufficient room to the private sector and subjected the latter to far too many regulations is plausible but over-simplified. A wide range of public investment activities is in fact supportive of and complementary to private effort. Public investment in irrigation, rural electrification, research and extension and rural infrastructure are crucial to raising agricultural production. These investments by their nature cannot be undertaken by the private sector. Public investment in electricity, rail transport and other major infrastructure also belong to this category. Moreover by creating demand for a variety of goods and services, public investment expands the growth opportunities of the private sector. The real issue is not whether there was too much public investment but whether the allocation of the investment as between various activities was consistent with the goals and whether the public sector performed its tasks efficiently.

Large parts of the private sector which still accounts for three-fourths of the country's output, have not been and still are not subject to state regulation. All of agriculture and rural economic activity, most of trade, road transport and personal services are in the private sector. Minimum wage laws, safety regulations, compulsory provident fund, health care and other requirements, which have to be met by establishments in the organized sector, do not apply to them. Most of these enterprises are not even required to register with the government; they do not need licences to be in business; they are free to produce what they want, by any means, on the scale they decide, and to sell their produce freely.

The regulatory system cannot be blamed for the poor performance of agriculture. State policy such as taxation, trade and exchange rate policy, support prices and compulsory

procurement and land laws—do affect the economic environment in which they operate. However, this is very different from the attempts at detailed and direct regulation of the
activities of individual enterprises which applied to organized industry and which affected performance.

The requirement of a licence for setting up and operating
an industry meant that until recently, a unit could produce
only those items and up to the limits specified in the licence;
substantial expansion of an existing unit as well as the setting up of a new unit required clearances from government;
the import of new equipment, raw materials and spares were
subject to government approval. Some scarce raw materials
were allocated by the government and there was formal or
informal control over the price at which products could be
sold. There was an active policy of discouraging big business
houses which was reinforced by the Monopolies and Restrictive Trade Practices Act of 1972. Securing the numerous
clearances required was enormously time-consuming and
often involved extra costs to get favourable and speedy
decisions.

Capacity licensing was supposed to be done on the basis
of targets set by the Planning Commission. The Commission
used fairly sophisticated input output models to fix targets
for major products or product categories consistent with the
objectives of the plan. However, these were not sufficiently
detailed as a guide to licensing. For example it is not enough
to specify the target for mild steel; one needs to know the
demand for specific categories of steel (e.g. bars and rods,
rails structural etc. of different sizes and specifications) in
order to decide what kind of extra capacities are needed.
This process of elaboration was left to committees consisting
of industry and government experts or simply to government departments. Since licensing was related to targets,
there were conflicts of interest between those who were already in business and those who wanted to enter the

business. The determination of targets itself was influenced by the interaction of these interests rather than on objective considerations.

In any case experience both in India and in the centrally planned economies, which sought to set and enforce detailed plan-wise targets, has shown that the agencies charged with the task do not get accurate and up-to-date information in the necessary detail; that individual enterprises can and do manipulate the information they provide the central authority if it suits their interest; and that it is impossible to establish an effective monitoring and enforcement system under such circumstances.

Furthermore, the various components of the control system came into being in a piecemeal fashion and were modified at various times to meet specific exigencies. Once in place, each element tended to acquire a certain autonomy of its own and changes needed to serve larger, unified goals were difficult to bring about. Consequently the components of the control regime were not always consistent in terms of promoting the larger goals. This necessarily reduced their effectiveness.

It is widely accepted that the present control system is not effective and may even be counter-productive. So is the desirability of dismantling the system to allow individual enterprises more space, greater freedom and flexibility in making their investment and production decisions in the light of market conditions. The market, it turns out, is a far more economical medium for signalling to all parties about the balance between supply and demand for particular goods and services in far greater detail and with far less bias than obtaining this information directly from producers and buyers.

This does not mean that markets invariably provide the right signals or that all the information necessary for decision can be obtained through markets. Markets are not always competitive and where they are not, the possibility of dominant producers or sellers manipulating prices exists. In any case decisions call for information about likely future demand, technology and alternatives both in the end uses and in ways of producing particular goods. The market is not the best place to get this kind of information.

More importantly the market tells us something *only* about activities which involve exchange among firms and between firms and consumers. A great deal of activity concerning the mobilization and utilization of resources lies *inside* enterprises (be they public or private) and other entities engaged in production and distribution. The collation and dissemination of information between different firms, the coordination of activities within each firm, and the systems of reward and punishment to ensure efficient production (i.e., getting the most out of resources available to the firm) are not mediated by the market. How these intra-enterprise problems are handled depends on the characteristics of entrepreneurs; their attitude to and relationship with professional managers and labour; and the internal organizational structure and the quality of management. These aspects are at least as important determinants of economic performance as the existence of efficient, competitive markets.

IMPLEMENTATION FAILURES

It is tempting to argue that failure lies not in the defective conception of strategy but in its poor implementation. There is ample *prima facie* evidence of the latter in the faulty preparation of projects, commissioning delays, inordinate cost escalations, low capacity use and the like; the abuse of the control system by bureaucracy and politicians; the lack of autonomy and accountability on the part of public enterprises; and the all-too-evident unwillingness to legislate measures to reduce inequalities and the ease with which enforcement of such measures can be thwarted. The system has also not shown much evidence of resilience in terms of learning from experience and adapting to changing circumstances. Indeed there is little sign of any serious and sustained interest among the executive agencies in this process.[4]

Central planning has had to function within the framework of a federal system with the respective spheres of the Centre and the states being clearly demarcated in the Constitution. In principle, the state governments are more or less free to determine policies and programmes in several sectors of the economy including agriculture and animal husbandry, irrigation, power, education, health and road transport. The Centre's power in respect of these sectors relates essentially to matters concerning inter-state relations. It also has the primary responsibility in respect of industry, atomic energy, shipping, railways and posts.

National economic planning pre-supposes an overall national consensus on objectives and priorities as well as effective instruments to ensure that programmes and policies are consistent with them. Differences are inevitable between the Centre and the states as well as among the states. The National Development Council was set up to serve as the forum through which a broad national consensus on the plan should be forged. In the initial stages the fact that the same political party held power both at the Centre and in practically all states facilitated the task of the Commission. But there were inevitable differences between the Centre and the states, and among the states, partly on substantive questions of objectives and strategy, but more importantly on the division of the financial resources among them. The distribution of financial powers—both regarding taxation and regulation of financial institutions—is decidedly in favour of the Centre. This has become the most effective instrument in the hands of the Centre in influencing state government policies and programmes.

The size of the plan (in terms of outlays) and the quantum of central assistance quickly emerged as major issues in the deliberations of the National Development Council. All parties involved have been consistently interested in a larger public sector plan; and the states as a group in raising the overall quantum of assistance to as high a level as possible. While both the Centre and the states usually agree to mount a substantial effort at economizing non-plan expenditures and mobilizing additional resources, these commitments are hardly binding.

The other important question, namely the allocation of central assistance over the five year plan as a whole among states, is also decided by the National Development Council. The Planning Commission has played a key role in evolving the criteria on which the central assistance to state plans is to be allocated among the states. In the early stages, this assistance, and the relative share of its loan and grant component, were linked to specific sectoral schemes/programmes ostensibly to ensure that national priorities were in fact observed by the states. But besides giving enormous scope for the Centre to interfere in the details of state plans, the system also became far too cumbersome and rigid, leading to a clamour for simplification. A major advance came with what has come to be known as the Gadgil formula by which the allocation of central plan assistance between states was linked to certain overall criteria including the size of the population. The relative backwardness of a state, special problems and the degree of tax effort have also been incorporated in the allocation criteria but population size continues to have largest weight.

The avowed aim of this simplification, to give states greater flexibility in the use of central assistance was, however, not fully achieved because the central ministries devised a new category of centrally sponsored schemes to promote programme concepts which the central ministries considered desirable. Also in the name of protecting the interests of priority sectors, a part of central assistance was earmarked for programmes in designated key sectors (of which power was important).

The Planning Commission had gone along with these dilutions of spirit and intent of the Gadgil formula if not actively promoted them. That the Commission acquiesced in the rapid growth of discretionary grants outside the plan and the Finance Commission awards, was a clear sign of weakening of the Planning Commission's influence over the allocation of resources at the command of the Centre. These tendencies had their roots partly in the propensity of the central ministries to seek greater influence on the states, especially as other avenues of such influence, both via the plan and through political mechanisms, were found to be weak and getting weaker.

In principle the detailed review of each state's programmes and priorities at the time of finalizing each five year plan along with the annual review of progress of plan schemes and resource mobilization conducted as part of the annual planning exercise, provide the occasion to persuade or pressure the errant states into taking corrective action. However, the review procedures are generally rather perfunctory, focussing far too much on outlays. In any case the Commission is not sufficiently well-informed to play an effective role. The states, which ultimately have to provide the necessary information for the Commission to form a judgement, are not particularly forthcoming.

The lack of relevant information from the states greatly restricts the Commission's ability to offer informed criticism or advice, assuming that the states are interested in either. The fact of course is that they are not. Even in the hey-day of the Congress, state governments were keen on getting as much central assistance as they could manage, with greater freedom to determine their own priorities. They were not particularly keen to implement commitments to mobilize additional resources. The Planning Commission could not prevent them from taking up several projects and programmes involving sizeable outlays outside the approved plan.

These departures may not be altogether undesirable if they were based on careful assessment of the problems and possibilities of individual states. But this was rarely the case. The states themselves do not have an effective mechanism for proper planning. The Planning Commission has long sought to convince the states into strengthening their planning agencies so that there will be a nodal point in each state which will perform the function of preparing coherent overall programmes, ensuring that their constituent elements are properly coordinated, and monitoring progress. While most states have set up Planning Boards or Commissions, they are for the most part ineffective in performing these functions. The status and power they command with their respective governments is far less than that of the national Planning Commission at the Centre. Conceding power to the Planning Board would change the internal balance of forces and the locus of power in the state government which obviously is not politically feasible.

Over the years, resistance among the states to the Centre's powers, and the way it is exercised, has grown. With the emergence of governments under opposition and regional parties in several states, the pressure to curb the power of the Centre and confer greater autonomy to the states has intensified. It is argued that

(a) an excessively large part of the potential tax and non-tax revenue of the states is concentrated with the Centre;

(b) in exercising its tax powers, the Centre uses stratagems (like increasing the price charged by enterprises rather than through taxes) which keep increments in revenue outside the divisible pool;

(c) the various formulae for devolution of central assistance do not cover borrowings in the open market;

(d) the Centre is increasingly encroaching into areas which constitutionally fall within the sphere of the states, in part through the mechanism of centrally sponsored schemes;

(e) these schemes are used to serve the political interests of the party in power at the Centre.

All these are invoked as powerful arguments in favour of giving much greater autonomy to states in the mobilization and use of resources.[5]

Many constraints on the Planning Commission's role vis-à-vis the states should not in principle be as severe as its role vis-à-vis the central ministries. After all the Commission is the creation of the Centre, the prime minister and key ministers are its members, and its charter is wide ranging. However, the central ministries have not been any more amenable to the discipline of planning than the states. It is true that inclusion in the five year plan has in general been a pre-requisite for projects of the ministries to be considered for financial allocation. There is in fact much discussion in the sectoral working groups and between the Commission and the ministries at the time of formulating each five year plan. It is at this time that the progress of past projects is reviewed and the allocation for these continuing projects as well as new projects is decided. Ministries invariably ask for more than what they can reasonably expect as their share within the projected resources for the plan as a whole. There is intensive bargaining and compromises are worked out even at this stage.

Once approved, the Planning Commission is supposed to review plan progress each year while deciding allocation in the annual budget; all new investment proposals are

62

supposed to be evaluated and cleared by the Commission before being approved, and indeed the Commission is to be consulted on all major policy matters. Except in one respect, namely investment approvals where the Commission's role has been strengthened by being made the agency to provide the techno-economic evaluation to the Public Investment Board, in most other respects its role has been less than effective.

Ministries are often unwilling to provide information on the status of major projects and programmes; several major changes in policy have been approved despite opposition from the Commission and sometimes (as in the case of bank nationalization and the nationalization of grain trade) without even consulting it. Many of the studies and reports which presage the recent shifts in the government's policy on fiscal matters, public sector, and regulation of the private sector took place outside the aegis of the Commission. The Commission has found it difficult to check the tendency of the central ministries to launch on programmes in spheres falling under the states and to provide large-scale discretionary assistance outside the plan. The Commission hardly comes into the picture in matters concerning pricing policy of public enterprises; it has also not been able to enforce fiscal discipline on the Centre any more than it has in the states.

The Planning Commission has no doubt provided an overall perspective of the main objectives and their implications in terms of the magnitude of expansion to be achieved in major sectors, and the investment requirement. The translation of these sectoral targets into detailed operational programmes (based on a proper technical and economic evaluation of alternatives), a coherent policy framework to induce the concerned enterprises (public and private) to adopt the socially desirable strategies to be regulated in the choice of location, scale technology and product mix of industrial projects—all this calls for strong organizations for sectoral planning and survey, design and engineering organizations to prepare specific projects. Interest in creating such organizations has been conspicuously weak or absent in the central ministries or in the large public sector enterprises concerned with major sectors like steel, energy, and transport. The Planning Commission has not shown serious and persistent interest in pursuing this task.

POLITICS AND PLANNING

In the Indian context, the political configurations have not been conducive to far-sighted planning.[6] The planners had from the beginning emphasized the primacy of rapid economic growth and ruled out any drastic redistribution of existing private wealth. Nevertheless even the limited extent of land reform considered necessary in the interests of both growth and equity, and the manner in which the resources required to finance growing public expenditures on development were to be raised predictably evoked strong resistance from those whose interests would be adversely affected. The inevitable conflict of interests among different classes and regions over the sharing of the benefits of public expenditure intensified as the scale of such expenditure expanded. The articulation of these conflicts and their resolution are fundamentally in the domain of politics.

The political process is sought to be regulated by the Constitution which defines the form, functions, modes of creation and control of various institutions constituting the government. The formal provisions, and certain unwritten conventions underlying them, are constantly evolving partly because of amendments to the statutes and partly as a result of judicial interpretation. The most important feature of the Constitution which bears on planning is the federal structure of government. The respective functions and powers of the Centre and the states have been defined in the Constitution in a manner that the Centre has much wider powers of taxation and borrowing relative to its functions.

The Centre has powers to levy income and corporate tax, central excise duties on production of a wide range of goods and services and customs duties. The proceeds of these taxes (except customs) are shared between the Centre and the states, the exact division being determined by the Finance Commission every five years. While the states have extensive taxation power, they have always complained that more important and lucrative revenue sources have been pre-empted by the Centre; that the states' share in central taxes is inadequate and that the Centre's control over government borrowing puts the states at an even greater disadvantage.

The truth is that the division of taxation powers and resource sharing between the Centre and the states has been a source of tension between the two; that the Centre can and does intervene even in areas falling exclusively under states' jurisdiction. This is done by offering sizeable financial inducements to persuade states to take up programmes conceived by the Centre and also by extending the concurrent list. This has significantly affected the priorities and allocations in the state plans. It has also considerably reduced the scope for states to try out innovative approaches, appropriate to their specific circumstances. The Centre-state conflicts on these matters have become sharper and more visible as electoral politics has become more competitive, and as the Congress lost the hegemony it enjoyed at the Centre and in most states.

The nature of conflicts and the ability of the State to resolve them depends crucially on the composition of the ruling classes and their ideology, the relative power of different constituents of these classes, the alliances and coalitions among them, and the way they seek to accommodate the claims of other groups in society.

At some risk of over-simplification, one could say that in many, if not most, countries which have reached a high level of development—be it capitalist or socialist—the capitalists and/or a managerial elite committed to modernization had acquired control of the State and used this power to resolve social conflicts more or less decisively in a way which favoured development. By contrast, in India since Independence no single homogeneous class has been able to acquire and retain control over State power.

The capitalists are clearly a powerful group but far from being the only one or even the most important one. In the absence of thorough-going land reforms, those with substantial holdings continue to be powerful in rural areas. Their sizeable presence in Parliament and state legislatures and their considerable influence over local power centres also makes them influential in the governance of the country. Apart from these the professionals, whose skills are essential to run a complex, modern polity, wield considerable power in government. Some scholars claim that these three classes constitute the "ruling coalition".[7]

Whether or not it is appropriate to view them as a "coalition" is debatable; at any rate, the interests of cultivators (predominantly rural) are not always the same as that of capitalist industrialists (predominantly urban) or of traders (who are everywhere). Caste affiliations and regional loyalties often cut across class boundaries even within these classes. Moreover, the coalition has to contend with the claims of other interest groups which may not have a direct influence in the government.

Despite all this, the propertied classes have effectively protected themselves against state actions which affect their interests adversely. This is evident from the fact that land ceilings, progressive direct taxation, inheritance taxes and other measures meant to reduce relative disparities in income and wealth have been reluctantly pursued and indifferently implemented. Large accumulations of wealth and incomes from illegal actions (such as tax evasion, smuggling, bribery and kickbacks) have been allowed to continue unchecked. Not only have various penal provisions in the statute book not been enforced, but efforts have been made from time to time to legalize them under various amnesty schemes.

The power to influence state policy is by no means confined to the classes mentioned above. The unionized segment of labour, which comprises only a small portion of the working class and is largely concentrated in urban, non-agricultural sectors, may not have significant direct power in government. But it is prominent in the opposition. They have shown their capacity to effectively press their claims through strikes and other means. The professional bureaucracy of the State also belongs to this class. Given the demonstrated ability of these groups to protect and improve their position, in both absolute and relative terms, it is arguable that these groups should be considered effectively a part of the ruling coalition.

The complex nature of the power-structure means that a great deal of the effort and resources of the State are spent in mediating the conflicts between different constituents of the coalition at the cost of mobilization and effective use of resources for development. This tendency is exacerbated because the ruling classes are feeling more and more compelled, largely due to the compulsions of mass politics, to take cognizance of the interests of the unorganized and poor segments of the population and seen to be doing something concrete to promote them. Though the poor are voiceless and not organized to press their claims directly, their numerical strength in the electorate has made political parties and individuals aspiring for power recognize their needs and to promise them jobs, subsidized food, subsidized credit and the like.

A deeper problem, and one which has come into prominence, arises from the fact that the working of the State is influenced not only by the interests of the 'ruling classes' but also by the interests of the functionaries (both political and bureaucratic) who run the State. In principle, as representatives of the people, legislatures lay down the goals of policy, pass laws and sanction funds to facilitate their realization. The translation of these into specific decisions and their implementation is done by the political executive through the bureaucracy. The interests of these two groups who man the organs of the state also significantly influence their performances and policies as well as the way they are implemented.

As public sector activities, developmental and non-developmental, have grown enormously in scale and complexity, the opportunities for patronage and corruption (via appointments, award of contracts, purchases of material and several other ways) have also grown. The vesting of many discretionary powers with the state functionaries vis-à-vis the private sector and the citizenry at large has further enhanced this potential. It did not take long for the political executives of the State to realize and exploit these opportunities of using their position to secure and nurture their support base. This was done by sanctioning projects benefiting particular localities or groups and interceding in decisions affecting particular interests or parties, by giving jobs, contracts, appointments to cooperatives, public corporations and other public bodies, to their immediate followers and party workers and by using all these as a source of funds to sustain party or personal political activity.

Investment decisions have got highly politicized as have the award of contracts. Both lead to wrong choice of location, scale technology and higher than necessary costs. Unmindful of budgetary constraints, more projects are sanctioned than can be completed with a reasonable lag. As a result all projects get delayed. Political pressures result in workers hired during construction of projects being regularized as employees in the operational phase. This has also led to overmanning and interference in operational decisions of public enterprises on award of construction contracts and hiring/promotions. Price adjustments have to be cleared with the minister/ministry officials. The interference is pervasive leading to severe erosion of incentives for efficient performance.

These tendencies have grown over time; contesting elections is expensive and the winners seek to recoup their costs during their tenure in office. As politics becomes more fluid the tenures get shorter and more precarious, the time horizons of political executives are shortened and the temptations to abuse public office intensified. A number of institutional mechanisms—permanent, professional civil service, Estimates Committees and Public Accounts Committees of Parliament and state legislatures, the Comptroller and Auditor General—have been devised to make sure that the executive uses public resources efficiently for the purposes for which they were sanctioned. However, all of them have been seriously compromised.

The political executive depends on the bureaucracy to carry out their programmes/policies. The bureaucracy is supposed not only to prefer considered advice on policies but also ensure probity and integrity in handling public resources. Gradually the political executives have found ways of 'softening' the bureaucracy into compliant agents—if not outright collaborators—of political functionaries in violating recognized norms. Partly for this reason, the politicians' ability to maintain the discipline of the civil service has been compromised. And they have been most reluctant to confront employees not only in matters of organizational discipline, but in respect of their collective demands on pay, benefit, service conditions etc. No party is keen to risk the consequences of taking on the organized strength of the bureaucracy.

The effectiveness of watch-dog institutions have also been reduced in a variety of ways: by controlling appointments to such offices; not providing sufficient resources or personnel with requisite expertise; failure to provide, fully and accurately, information sought by these agencies; and calculated laxity in taking follow up action on the findings and recommendations of these bodies. Much of the information is not in the public domain. Either it is not made available or is 'classified' to restrict access. This makes it difficult for interested citizens and non-government organizations to pursue such matters.

5

Structural Reforms: A Critical Appraisal

It is hardly surprising given this historical and political background that the government could not muster the foresight and the firmness to avert the foreign exchange and fiscal crises which were building up during the 1980s. It was only when the foreign exchange situation became desperate that the government was compelled by circumstances to act. In the process it had to recognize that the crises were deep-seated and required corrective action over a very wide front. Thanks to donor pressure a fairly wide ranging set of reforms was initiated and is being pursued since June 1991.

The results of the first two years of structural adjustment are mixed. A substantial reduction in the fiscal deficit of the Centre, the stability of the rupee even after making it convertible, the increase in foreign exchange reserves to a reasonable level and the near-halving of the inflation rate are striking achievements. But closer examination suggests that the achievements are much less solid than they appear at first sight.

The reduction in the fiscal deficit is confined to the central budget. Actual deficits as percentage of the GDP have exceeded targets and it seems unlikely that the reduction targeted for 1993-94 will be realized. Whatever reduction has occurred is largely due to a reduction in the central budgetary support to the plan (including state plans) and trimming the public sector plan outlay. The finances of the states and public enterprises do not show any sign of improvement. It is also arguable that the drop in the inflation rate is as much due to favourable harvests—which have nothing to do with the reforms—as to the cut back in the fiscal deficit. The latter, in so far as it is the result of slowing down plan outlays rather than cutting down non-development spending, may well prolong the adjustment phase.

Export performance has been much poorer than expected. Export earnings in foreign exchange terms rose by less than 3 per cent a year during the first two years against a projected 15 per cent a year. There has been a remarkable turn around during 1993-94, with exports growing by 20 per cent (in dollar terms) during the first eight months. Whether this will be sustained in the coming years remains to be seen. If it is, the reform would have achieved one of its main objectives.

If nevertheless foreign exchange reserves have risen to over $10 billion, and the exchange rate has been relatively steady, it is largely because of sizeable receipts on accounts of the IMF and fast-disbursing World Bank assistance and more importantly to the stagnation of imports which in turn reflect the virtual stagnation of industrial output and of investment. The GDP growth as well as industrial growth in the last three years have remained well below the levels recorded in the eighties.

The difficulties in getting through even the proposed cuts in food and fertilizer subsidies not to mention relaxing the conditions for exit, reorganization of public enterprises and such more basic reforms, clearly shows the government is simply not strong enough to carry through the reform package whose elements are unpalatable to one or other of the politically powerful interest groups.

Viewed in a longer term perspective the reform package

is derived from a particular diagnosis of the structural problems of the Indian economy and the appropriate remedies. While there would be no disagreement on the need for basic reforms and several of the proposed measures, considerable difference of opinion exists as to the scope, emphasis and effectiveness of the changes in policy with reference to foreign trade and investment, measures to reduce the fiscal deficit and dismantling of controls. At the same time the content of policy changes remains hazy in such critical areas as public enterprise reform and privatization. Other aspects (e.g. agricultural development or getting the spirit of the reforms to permeate to the states) still remain to be addressed seriously.

FOREIGN TRADE AND INVESTMENT POLICIES

Import liberalization and opening the doors to free flow of foreign capital and technology which are central to the reform remain controversial. Some economists have argued that the liberalization policy of the 1980s aggravated the external deficit by stimulating faster import growth. A substantial part of imports is being used directly or indirectly to support luxury consumption. A tight control of luxury-related imports, according to this perception, would bring down import requirements without affecting the growth of the economy. Closer examination does not lend support to this view.

In fact, the liberalization of the 1980s was limited in scope; and imports of items (e.g. equipment) covered by liberalization did not show acceleration. Moreover, though the overall output of goods and services in the economy as a whole seems to have grown considerably faster during the eighties than before, total imports did not. The consequences of large imports for defence and other non-developmental purposes in the early part of the decade financed by suppliers credits seems to have been a far more important contributing factor.

Some of the imports no doubt go directly or indirectly into luxury consumption (such as private automobiles, two-wheelers, consumer electronic equipment, refrigerators, washing machines and other such durable consumer goods, synthetic fibres and the like). But the magnitude of legal imports in this category has been much smaller than claimed by some; and certainly small in relation to the magnitude of the deficit which has to be made up. In any case reducing imports of materials and components used for luxury goods would mean sharp cut backs in production and employment of the domestic industry producing such goods: hardly a palatable outcome.

Reducing imports is therefore hardly likely to reduce the pressure on balance of payments without adversely affecting the overall level of output and employment. On the contrary going back to the earlier policy (of keeping a tight lid on the level of imports, permitting each licencee to import only the specified commodities up to specified limits, and not allowing any sale or exchange of licences) will prevent the economy from realizing the potential for growth. This is part of the case for full import liberalization. But if liberalization succeeds in releasing the latent dynamic impulses in the economy, import requirements would increase and, at least for a while, grow faster than in the recent past.

Since imports cannot be brought down, export growth is critical. It is estimated that sustained increase in export earnings at the rate of 15–20 per cent a year is essential to sustain, over the long term, a reasonably high rate of overall GDP growth (say around 6 per cent per annum) with a viable balance of payments under a liberal trade and exchange rate regime. It is difficult to fault the government's efforts to increase the profitability of exports vis-à-vis production for the

Remittances

domestic market by devaluation, removal of export restrictions, freedom to import materials, equipment and technology and reduced tariff on imported materials. Skepticism on the ground that India's export prospects will be severely restricted by the growing protectionism of the developed countries is hardly convincing: India's exports constitute a minuscule fraction of world exports and even with a 15 per cent annual growth India would remain a relatively minor presence in world trade. There is more substance to the argument that making exports more profitable alone will not suffice to guarantee faster export growth.

The poor export performance during the last two years bears testimony to this. Total exports in fact declined in this period. While part of this ought to be explained by the drastic reduction in trade with East Europe, the 10 per cent growth in exports to other countries is not particularly impressive and certainly not adequate. The various general measures need to be followed up with efforts to identify sectors with relatively high potential for export growth and programmes geared to upgrade technology, designs and quality in production; market and survey promotion programmes to enter or expand presence in large and growing foreign markets; and induce the relevant industries and trade to have an active and far-sighted commitment to exports. These efforts are as yet rather weak.

Even with such a high rate of export growth, there will be a transition period (lasting perhaps a decade or even more) during which the country will have to depend to a substantial, and even increasing, extent on other sources such as the remittances of Indians working abroad, foreign aid and investment. The oil boom in West Asia, and consequently the demand for immigrant workers has more or less reached a plateau. The prospects for the growth of remittances are therefore bleak. The outlook for increased aid from official bilateral and multilateral agencies is also generally recognized to be dim. Further recourse to commercial loans, NRI deposits and other forms of borrowing is undesirable because they tend to be much more expensive and sometimes volatile. That leaves us with direct foreign investment.

The official aid agencies (especially the Bank and the Fund) place a great deal of emphasis on larger inflows of foreign private investment and the need to create conditions favourable to attract such investment. The Indian government has not till recently been enthusiastic about private foreign investment and opposition to multinationals remains strong. This attitude is the result of several factors including memories of colonial rule and foreign exploitation, apprehensions that the interests of foreigners (especially the huge multinational corporations) may conflict with our national interests, the difficulties of enforcing MNC compliance with national laws (dramatized by the Bhopal gas leak case) as well as the numerous instances of multinationals influencing the internal politics of countries where they operate. The proponents of MNCs argue that these fears are misplaced, that the world has changed a great deal since 1950, that MNCs are a potentially rich vehicle for bringing the latest technology to India and helping us take advantage of the global market, and that equity investment is less burdensome on the balance of payments.

Opinions on this matter differ sharply: at the very least one must guard against oversimplification of the issues involved. The experience of Japan and Korea show that MNC presence is not necessary to build a dynamic and technologically sophisticated economy. The willingness of MNCs to transfer up-to-date technology cannot be taken for granted. Control of technology and the means to use it are powerful instruments which can be used for political influence if not control. At present much of modern technology and innovation happen to be in the developed countries. And they are seeking to impose more onerous conditions (through, for example, widening the scope of Intellectual Property Rights, tightening terms of access to technology and restrictions on technology transfer with potential military applications) for access to these techniques by developing countries. In an era where technological change is taking place at a phenomenal pace, it is particularly important for countries like India to develop the indigenous base for adapting and improving known technology and for developing new technologies appropriate to their needs.

Foreign private capital does not of course necessarily mean only multinationals: most of the private foreign investment in China, for example, is by overseas Chinese with considerable industrial experience. The Indian situation is different. While there are successful Indian businessmen abroad (some with large scale operations), much of the capital believed to have been accumulated illegally by Indian citizens is held not only by the industrial entrepreneurial class but also by traders, politicians and bureaucrats. At the same time there are a large number of Indian professionals abroad with the knowledge and expertise in sophisticated new areas who may not have the resources or the experience to set up large enterprises. This raises questions of propriety about condoning illegal accumulations of foreign balances (and even more about offering incentives to woo these funds) because their money is valuable. In any case mobilizing such resources for productive investments requires a different kind of approach and arrangements than in the case of MNCs or in the case of private foreign investment in China.

The argument that complete integration with the world economy based on free trade and free flow of capital and technology is essential to healthy industrial growth is also simplistic. A freer flow of knowledge and technique is indeed essential. The world is experiencing changes of phenomenal scope and speed, and a degree of selectivity is essential in determining what products and processes are appropriate in the Indian context. It is necessary to keep in view the ability of existing industries to adapt to the changes without causing serious dislocations; the potential they may have for aggravating environmental problems; the country's resource endowments relative to population; and the kind of consumption patterns which are sustainable for the mass of the people over the long run. Advertisements and mass communication through the open skies are powerful inducers of demand and this is reason enough for not leaving the choices wholly to the market place.

Furthermore, given the speed of technical progress, large scale technology imports freely permitted can create a prolonged, if not perpetual, dependence on imported technology. The recently concluded negotiations on intellectual property rights are designed to meet the concerns of the developed countries rather than protect the interests of the third world (especially in respect of access to the developed country markets for labour intensive manufactures and to technology). India, and developing countries generally, have been more or less powerless to safeguard their interests to any significant degree. It may be conceded that India's interests would be better served by being part of a multilateral world trade system than staying out of it. But immediate compulsions cannot be allowed to detract from purposive action to enhance indigenous technological capacity over the long run. This calls for a discriminating policy on technology imports backed by indigenous organizations for absorbing the techniques, adapting and improving on them.

The success of countries like Japan and Korea in mastering a wide range of sophisticated technology and building the indigenous capability for improving on them—which is at the root of their miraculous performance—was not the result of laissez faire and free trade but rather of conscious state policy for technology import, adaptation and fresh innovation implemented in collaboration with industry.[1] The success of this policy—in terms of the range and sophistication of technological capability as well as the speed with which it was accomplished—has important lessons for India and for the debate on liberalization. This aspect is not receiving anywhere near the attention it deserves in the agenda of reform.

FISCAL ADJUSTMENT

A sizeable part of the reduction of the central government fiscal deficit during the last two years is due to the reduction in food and fertilizer subsidies, and containing the growth of non-development expenditures. The reduction in subsidies, though smaller than visualized, is still substantial. The level of defence expenditures has also remained more or less constant in the last two years. Both are to be welcomed. But whether this can be sustained and carried further in the face of strong political pressures is a moot question.

The other major factors contributing to the reduction in the Centre's deficit are disinvestment of government holdings in the equity capital of public undertakings and a substantial reduction in the volume of resources made available through the central budget for development programmes of public enterprises and smaller increases in the central assistance to the states. The former, amounting as it does to a sale of capital assets, provides only a temporary relief; and its wisdom is open to question. The policy of limiting the budget support to public undertakings and forcing them to rely on their own resources and their direct borrowings from the market is a step in the right direction.

The fact of the matter is that the states' financial position is weaker and has been deteriorating even faster than that of

79

the Centre. There has been a progressive decline in the states' share in the total approved outlay between successive plans, and their share in actual plan outlays has fallen even more. The states are responsible for agriculture, irrigation, road, electricity, education, health and other programmes which are crucial to overall growth and to the welfare of the poor. Resource constraints have already led to a serious deterioration in the quality of services provided by past investments. Any erosion in their capacity to make fresh investments to expand and improve these facilities will have serious adverse consequences for overall growth.

It is of course true that there is vast scope for releasing more resources for development by cutting down subsidies on services and facilities provided by the states. As we have noted earlier the magnitude of explicit and implicit subsidies on irrigation, electricity, urban amenities, road transport, education, health etc. given by the states is much larger than the food fertilizer and export subsidies provided by the Centre. There is also considerable room for general improvement in the efficacy of public spending and on plan programmes, specially by rationalizing programmes to avoid overlapping and duplication and by better planning of both the scale and content of programmes in different regions in the light of their specific needs and possibilities.

These problems are not getting the emphasis and attention they deserve. The Planning Commission, which ought to be concerned with these larger, more basic and long term issues, has chosen not to raise them or to force a discussion in the NDC as to the imperative need for states both to mobilize resources, and to use available resources more efficiently. It is naive to imagine that exhortations or even pressure by the Centre to raise electricity and irrigation rates, bus fares and so on will make the states act; or that privatization will solve the problem.

To a significant degree deterioration in the states'

resource position is due to the policies of the Centre, especially the rise in the price of goods and services rendered by central Government enterprises. Similarly, poor targeting and waste in anti-poverty and rural development programmes are largely the result of fragmented and ad hoc proliferation of programmes initiated by the Centre. The states are under constant pressure, in this age of competitive populism, to extend "welfare" type programmes even at the cost of productive investment and to spread resources thinly over large areas and numerous projects. Leakages and corruption in the collection of revenue and in the implementation of programmes have become an integral part of the political fund-raising and patronage networks. Raising utility charges is universally unpopular among politicians. Necessary reforms in all these spheres is impossible without a political consensus between parties and between the Centre and the states.

But instead of building on the rather broad consensus which existed on the relaxation of controls and taking advantage of the very tight financial position of the states to evolve a programme for improving the finances of electricity, irrigation and transport, the Centre announced its package without any consultation. The package was presented as if it was the only one or the best of available choices, with strident claims as to the speed and magnitude of the expected results. Nor was there adequate effort to educate public opinion, and develop a broad based support for the package after it was presented. Indeed opportunities to forge such a consensus have not only been missed, but on occasion actively subverted.

Thus the committee of chief ministers appointed by the National Development Council last year (and consisting of all shades of political opinion) recognized the need for all round austerity and made a number of recommendations to this end. A far-sighted leadership would have used this as

81

the starting point to evolve a broad political consensus on ways to reduce subsidies, to control expenditures and make more effective use of resources. Instead the immediate interests of the Centre in avoiding an impending confrontation with its employees was considered overriding. The Chief Ministers' report was not even seriously discussed by the NDC. Instead the decision to grant an increase in dearness allowance and appoint a new pay commission has made the task of fiscal adjustment even more difficult.

REFORM OF PUBLIC ENTERPRISES

Reform of the PSUs is largely focussed on disinvestment as a means of tiding over the fiscal crisis. This is an extremely narrow and short-sighted approach. Quite apart from the problem of ensuring that disinvestment is made transparently and on fair terms, the sale of assets does not really add in any sustained manner to the resources available to the budget. It cannot make a lasting impact on the budget.

Nor is it clear that once the private sector acquires a significant stake in PSU equity, there will automatically be strong and effective pressures for improving efficiency, unless, of course, the intention is to hand over management to private share holders and allow them to function autonomously. Such a change seems unlikely so long as the government or the public financial institutions own the majority of equity. The real issue is autonomy of the enterprises, i.e., freedom from government interference in firm-specific policies and detailed decisions concerning the operation of each firm, along with a credible mechanism for monitoring overall performance and making the management accountable for its performance. It is autonomy of enterprises consistent with accountability, and *not* ownership, which is the crucial issue.

This requires first of all that political control and parliamentary oversight must be strictly limited to matters of broad policy in respect of a particular sector. The fact that the State or its institutions 'own' a substantial chunk or even the bulk of the equity does not mean that the political executive or the ministry should interfere in firm-specific policies. Divorce between ownership and management is the norm even in the private sector of developed economies. And the scale, range and complexity of some large corporations in the world is greater than that of the Indian public sector taken as a whole! This has not prevented these enterprises from being innovative and profitable. The connection between ownership and management control is overdrawn.

In the interests of greater transparency in the working of public enterprises, it is essential to change the format of their accounts to indicate explicitly and separately those activities/expenditures which they are expected to incur for purposes which have nothing to do with efficient performance of the main tasks of production and distribution. This includes costs on account of PSUs being forced to give permanent employment to people who were engaged in construction or otherwise for work which is not functionally related to its operation; the cost of being a "model" employer calling for payment of wages, amenities etc., on a higher scale than is normally expected of similar private enterprises; the cost of being required to subsidize particular segments of the operation or particular classes of consumer, without the power to charge higher prices on other operations and consumers. All these must be explicitly indicated and netted while assessing the financial performance of PSUs; and the losses involved must be borne by the general budget rather than by the enterprises.

A sense of stake and loyalty among managers and workers is of course critical. But it is not achieved by the kind of detailed oversight and interference now being exercised by the executive and the legislature. Indeed these have had quite the opposite effect. We need to explore other means such as employee stock holding, a high level of internal communication and a drastic reduction in profit-making by manipulation of government policy. Government intervention in public enterprises, as in the private sector, will have to be strategic, related to long term goals in the realization of which the government and the enterprises work in close consultation and collaboration. Managements and workers have to be judged on the basis of their ability to realize broad goal of returns on investment and growth/diversification, the reward system being in part related to the success in achieving these broad goals.

The active involvement of workers of public undertakings is critical for the success of the reforms. The prospects of securing it are dim if large-scale retrenchment is viewed as a pre-requisite for reform. The hardening of the budget constraint creates conditions under which labour can be made aware that continued, large losses are unsustainable. Labour must then be made conscious that the plant/industry can do much better with available resources in terms of capacity use, more economical use of materials and proper recovery of dues from users of their product. The aim should be to secure workers' cooperation in exploiting these potentials on the basis of an explicit understanding that the gains from efficiency improvement will be shared with workers in such a way that retrenchment is kept to a minimum and phased over a period of time and necessary retraining and redeployment of personnel being made an integral part of the package. In cases where the State wants to quit a field altogether, alternative ways of divestment—professional management contracts, worker management and outright sale—should be considered in the light of circumstances specific to each case.

PRIVATIZATION

On the broader issue of privatization, the government's policies remain ill-defined, often ambiguous. The compulsions on account of the severe shortage of resources facing the public sector have forced the government to consider letting the private sector in infrastructure areas. Several state governments have declared their intention to pursue this option and the 1993-94 budget indicated that the Electricity Act will be suitably amended to facilitate private investment. The idea is to attract private investment in electricity generation with a promise of guaranteed return. But the details have not been thought through and many questions remain unanswered.

Take the case of power: if the private power plants are to be guaranteed a certain return, will there be any mechanism to ensure that the costs are 'reasonable'? If the State Electricity Boards (SEBs) are to purchase power from the private sector at guaranteed prices, without revising the rates charged to consumers, the already bad financial position of SEBs can only suffer further deterioration. Is there the willingness to revise rates charged to consumers so that this situation does not arise? If on the other hand, the private sector is to be allowed to sell power directly, how is this to be managed? How will the grid be managed? Is it considered desirable/necessary to regulate the level and structure of rates charged by the private sector? If so, on what criteria and through what mechanisms will rates, and rate revisions, be regulated? These questions are relevant for any large-scale privatization of infrastructure and social services.

The enlargement in the spheres open to the private sector and the dismantling of the control regime leaves open the question of the relation between the State and the private sector. There is a view, and this comes closest to the traditional laissez faire view, that the State should confine itself to maintaining law and order, providing basic education, health services and other (unspecified) infrastructure; and protect the public from malpractices and fraud from private enterprise through protective (prudential) regulations effectively enforced. In this view all regulation like factory laws, measures meant to protect worker's rights, laws relating to trade unions should also be done away with or at any rate drastically reduced and simplified so that enterprise will be free and have the maximum flexibility to exploit emerging opportunities for expanding output and raising productivity.

The issue really is not whether the State should intervene, but where and how. To say that the State should not interfere with the market mechanism in determining prices, or control the choice of technology, scale, location, production pattern and other facets of resource allocation in the private sector or for that matter in public enterprises is not to say that the State should not intervene at all. By now it is widely recognized that the economic "miracles" of Korea, Taiwan, or for that matter Japan are the product of purposive intervention of the State not only in maintaining macro-economic stability, but by selecting a few strategic thrust areas for long term development, identifying promising entrepreneurs and helping them acquire and master the know-how and establish efficient productive facilities; and devising effective monitoring and incentive mechanisms to ensure performance.

There were of course special circumstances, deriving partly from history and partly from the features specific to their social-political configurations, which made all this feasible in east Asia. In all these cases, land reforms had effectively altered the power relations within rural areas as well as between rural areas and the rest of society; political power was with an identifiable group committed to modernization, and this group acquired a hegemonic position vis-à-vis other interests, including the capitalists; they have been authoritarian regimes which kept labour under control; and while actively collaborating with the private entrepreneurs there was not much doubt as to who was in charge. That east Asian societies are relatively more homogeneous socially is also believed to be a contributory factor. It is not authoritarian per se (there are far too many instances of despotisms which have led to moribund and stagnant societies) but the ability of political authority to exploit internal configurations and external opportunities so flexibly and effectively which marks out East Asia as unique.

The situation in India clearly does not permit anything like a replication of the east Asian model. But it is important to rethink how the State can enter into a more creative interaction with key interest groups in society so that the economy may become more buoyant without compromising on its obligation to protect the disadvantaged and the destitute, and ensure a minimum standard in respect of basic needs to all segments of the population.

AGRICULTURE

A major lacuna in the on-going reform effort is in respect of agriculture. India being a low income country, increase in income is likely to generate significant increases in demand for food. If investment and industrial growth are to be sustained at significantly higher levels without giving rise to larger food imports and/or inflation—both of which will create pressures on the balance of payments—it is imperative that the rate of agricultural growth must be stepped up well above the past trend rate of 2.6 per cent a year. This is recognized in the recent paper on economic reforms published by the central government but it has little to say on exactly how the current policies are to be recast to achieve the goal.

The reformulation of agricultural policy raises difficult

political problems: on the one hand cutting the fiscal deficit without affecting the resources available for investment compels a reversal of the policy of subsidizing the supply of agricultural inputs. Since the magnitude of the subsidies and the number of people who will be adversely affected by their removal is large, opposition to this course is understandably strong. These inputs are being used less efficiently than is possible with known technology and this tendency is actually encouraged by the policy of 'cheap inputs'. This has not made much of an impression on the farm lobby. The latter's resistance to phasing out subsidies is sought to be rationalized on the ground that the prices of farm produce relative to that of manufactures are unfavourable and have been falling.

It had been suggested that the difficulty could be overcome if removal of farm input subsidies were combined with free trade in agricultural commodities.[2] At present the prices of some farm products (notably foodgrains) are well below prices in the world market, while others (e.g. edible oils and sugar) are above world prices. Allowing free trade in agricultural products is expected to result both in a higher average level of prices in the domestic market and a substantial change in the structure of relative prices. The former, the argument goes, will neutralize the effect of removal of subsidies, release more resources for public investment in agricultural infrastructure even as the improvement in the agricultural sector's terms of trade will stimulate larger private investment in agriculture. The change in relative prices is also expected to grow by inducing shifts in the pattern of use of productive resources in agriculture that are more in line with the country's comparative advantage in the world market. All of this will cumulatively lead to faster growth.

The above line of reasoning, which is advanced by the World Bank, is however unlikely to be acceptable either to the farm lobby (which welcomes higher output prices but not free imports of farm produce or a significant reduction in input subsidies) or to the urban population and the rural poor who depend on purchased food (because the policy would result in significant rise in domestic foodgrain prices). This political difficulty apart, the impact of these changes in prices, by themselves, on the growth of aggregate output is unlikely to be significant or sustained. The fact remains that any step-up in agricultural growth is contingent on investment in developing land and water resources, in generating better varieties and cropping practices, and in getting farmers to use all inputs more efficiently.

Over the long run a larger volume of investment (both public and private) is necessary to achieve all this. But it is also true that the resources (especially in the public sector) currently devoted to agriculture can be used to much greater effect. These include tighter planning of irrigation projects; stricter control and monitoring of implementation; greater attention to improvements in the management of public irrigation systems for more efficient use of water; improvement in the organization and management of research to make it more accountable and responsive to farmers' needs; and reducing duplication and waste in respect of soil conservation, social forestry, minor irrigation, rural infrastructure and other elements of 'rural development'. All this calls for major changes in the way public investment decisions are made and monitored; as well as greater consultation with, and involvement of, the beneficiaries in planning, implementation and management of facilities. Effective decentralization of responsibility along with the resources for local level development works also has potentially a crucial role in improving the efficacy of public spending on rural development.

Without tackling these fundamental issues of institutional reform, an increase in public sector outlays is unlikely to accomplish any dramatic improvement in agricultural performance. The recent constitutional amendment on Panchayati Raj marks an important step towards democratic decentralization. But the implementation of this reform on the ground in all the states faces strong resistance from those who benefit from the present centralized arrangement. It calls for a degree of seriousness and persistence which is not yet in evidence. Other elements of institutional reform are not yet even on the agenda.

6

Conclusion

What role if any should planning have in a new arrangement? There is a continuing need for reviewing the overall trends in the economy, anticipating emerging opportunities and potential bottlenecks in the medium and long-term perspective, and organizing action ahead of time to exploit the opportunities (and to avoid problems). The rapidity with which technology is changing and the implications of projected developments in terms of claims on non-renewable natural resources, dependence on imports and environmental impact, heighten rather than lessen, the need for a coherent long-term view as a basis for policy.

For this reason it is a matter of regret that in the context of the current crisis, the Planning Commission has abdicated its role in focussing on the adequacy and impact of the reform package and the inconsistencies and gaps which need attention from the medium and long-term viewpoint. Equally regrettable is the failure of the central government to utilize the Commission, which is the most effective bridge between the Centre and states, to get a wider consensus on the reforms. The Finance Ministry is simply not equipped for these tasks and there is no other institution in government which can provide these essential inputs for structural reform.

The Planning Commission must continue to play an important role though of a rather different kind and at a much higher level of sophistication than before. In the first place the responsibility for planning and implementation of public sector programmes needs to be greatly decentralized even as institutional mechanisms are created to ensure that the decentralized agencies are accountable for their performance. Decentralization consists of three distinct elements. First, greater functional autonomy for public enterprises responsible for infrastructure services, and basic inputs (e.g. power) in respect of investment, technology, production and pricing decisions, subject only to broadly indicated policy guidelines and subject to regulation by autonomous authorities (e.g. public utility lands). This would mean a much greater role for financial institutions and independent regulatory agencies in respect of public utilities pricing, in defining and enforcing educational standards and the like. Second, the tendency of the Centre to undertake programmes on its own or to induce states to take up programmes of its conception in spheres falling under states should be curbed. The third, perhaps most far reaching of all, is decentralization of the responsibility for local development works to local government institutions.

At present perhaps up to one-fifth of the total public sector outlay is on such schemes, which are at once numerous, characterized by a great deal of overlap, and implemented by different agencies. Their scope and content is often decided by the Centre with little flexibility for the states, not to speak of local authorities, to decide the content in the light of local needs and potentials. Many of these programmes are supposed to benefit specific target groups of poor people/ regions. But the effectiveness of targeting is known to be very weak.

There is a strong case for pooling all or the bulk of resources devoted to local development (including targeted poverty alleviation programmes) and dividing the pool into two parts: the first consisting of programmes to ensure basic facilities in education, health, water supply and sanitation; the second of programmes to develop local productive resources in agriculture, livestock and small industry. The former could be distributed to the states and then to districts, in proportion to the magnitude of the deficit between the specified minimum standard in respect of each facility and the facilities currently available. Conditions can be attached regarding the level of local contributions towards maintaining the facilities. In respect of the second category the pool should be distributed between the state and then the district in each state in proportion to the number of poor people, the number of unemployed and, if need be, the scheduled caste/tribe population. (Alternatively a part could be earmarked for the benefit of the last category.) This way a substantial part of the targeting problem will be taken care of and the local authority will have the freedom to decide on the content of local programmes. The resources will also be more efficiently used especially where a democratically elected Panchayati Raj system is in operation.

Such an approach would call for changes in the existing planning set up. On the one hand the level of information, knowledge and expertise available to the planning agencies both at the Centre and the states should be substantially improved. The planning function needs to be strengthened not only at the level of the central or the state planning agencies, but much more in the functional departments. The executive departments of government, besides taking care of large national/state level projects, would help local authorities with relevant expertise, (including information on the experiences of other districts/states in planning local development) and ensure that local works are informed by and linked to developments over a wider area. Decentralization of local development will also reduce the direct responsibility of line departments in preparing, implementing and managing schemes.

Planning has clearly to go considerably beyond preparing macro-economic projections and determining the size and allocations of the public sector plan. Far greater attention should be given to evolving coherent long-term programmes and policies and to the problems of detailed planning, project preparation and technology development in respect of key sectors. This calls for very different kinds of expertise and organizations than are currently available.

Besides building up such capability at the state level— where a good part of planning for agriculture, electricity, roads etc., has to be done—the government has to play an active role in creating an atmosphere conducive to the growth of specialized organizations; in bringing the industrial enterprises (irrespective of whether they are in the public or private sector), industry associations, private design and engineering organizations, universities and research institutions into an effective interaction; facilitating wider, quicker diffusion of knowledge about existing and prospective technology; promoting technology assessment and development keeping in view the needs and constraints of the country; and promoting close interaction between sectoral enterprises, enterprises in related sectors, design engineers, technologists and research institutions.

Greater freedom for the private industrial sector must go with mechanisms for interchange of information and creative interaction between related industries and public and private agencies which are supposed to help in absorbing and developing technology. Institutions for better management of land, water and credit are critical to realizing the full potential of available agricultural technology. The State can and should play a very active role in both these spheres as well as in supporting result-oriented research for developing improved/new technologies in select important areas. Here

94

again devising appropriate institutional mechanisms is the central problem.

To sum up, the elimination of all domestic economic controls and a liberalization of external economic relations are not sufficient conditions for making India a dynamic economy. The wisdom of allowing free import of technology and foreign capital is questionable. A strong, far-sighted and sustained programme to enhance indigenous capability for absorbing imported technology, for adapting and improving such techniques and for developing new technology calls for greater attention and emphasis. It is of course essential to dismantle the system of direct controls to enable enterprises, both private and public, to function with greater freedom and flexibility. This does not mean that the State has to be passive; it has to intervene strategically, indirectly and at fewer points. The State will have to play a more active and effective role in defining and enforcing the rules of the game by all economic agents; it will have to continue to take direct responsibility in agriculture and industry; and it will have to continue programmes to help the poorer, more vulnerable segments of the population acquire the means for a reasonable basic level of living.

Reorienting the foci and modes of State intervention is but part of the solution. Just as important is an improvement in the efficacy of the State and its agencies in implementing its programmes and policies. This calls for major changes in the way the State's activities (including its enterprises) are organized and managed. A reduction in the extent of central government interference in shaping priorities and programmes of state governments; encouraging states to reshape and reorganize their programmes in view of their specific circumstances; decentralization of responsibility for local development works to democratically elected agencies at the district level and below; devising efficiency-inducing incentive systems; more objective and transparent procedures for clearance of projects and monitoring their progress are some of the reforms needed. Except for democratic decentralization, a systemic change of such proportions is not on the active agenda. And without substantial improvement in efficiency and public accountability of state agencies, the impact of the structural reform on overall growth or on the efficacy of poverty alleviation programmes is likely to be slower and smaller than promised.

Tables

TABLE 1

Selected indicators of overall economic performance in India 1950-51 to 1990-91

	1950-51	1960-61	1970-71	1980-81	1990-91
Gross domestic product at factory cost (Rs. crores at constant 1980-81 prices)	42871	62904	90426	122427	209791
Per capita net national product at 1980-81 prices	1127	1350	1520	1630	2199
Index of agricultural production (1969-71=100)	58.5	86.7	111.5	135.3	192
Index of industrial production (1980-81=100)	18.3	36.2	65.3	100	212.6
Wholesale price index (1981-82=100)	16.9	19.6	35.3	91.1	182.7

Source: Govt. of India, *Economic Survey*, 1992-93.

TABLE 2
Savings and capital formation

	1950-51 to 1954-55	1960-61 to 1964-65	1970-71 to 1974-75	1980-81 to 1984-85	1985-86 to 1989-90	1990-91 to 1992
Economy as a whole						
1. Gross domestic capital formation as % of GDP	9.46	15.24	17.44	21.1	23.76	25.9
2. Gross domestic savings as % of GDP	9.2	12.9	16.6	19.7	21.3	23.9
3. (2) as % of (1)	97	84	95	93	89	92
Public Sector						
4. Gross capital formation as % of GDP	2.96	7.46	7.24	10.22	11.14	10
5. Gross savings as % of GDP	1.64	3.04	2.98	3.68	2.34	1.4
6. (5) as % of (4)	55	40	41	36	21	14

GOI, *Economic Survey*, 1992-93.

TABLE 3

India's balance of payments 1960-61 to 1990-91 (million US$)

	1960-61	1970-71	1980-81	1985-86	1989-90
Imports (cif)	2323	2435	15862	17298	24411
Exports (fob)	1325	1873	8316	9463	16955
Invisibles					
Receipts	546	661	7449	6437	7498
Payments	372	711	1997	3470	6883
Current A/c balance	-824	-594	-2095	-4844	-6836
Net capital transactions*	+169	-616	-1243	+2239	+3094
External assistance	+539	+991	+2186	+2028	+3002
IMF	-	+100	+499	-	+740
Reserve change**	+124	+118	+652	+577	
Foreign exchange reserves at end year	637	975	6823	6520	3962

GOI, *Economic Survey*, 1992-93.

* (+) denotes net inflow (–) net outflow.

** (+) denotes depletion of reserves.

99

TABLE 4
Trends in Indian agriculture, 1950-51 to 1991-92

	1950-51	1960-61	1970-71	1980-81	1990-91
			Absorption of inputs		
Net area sown (m hectares)	118.7	133.2	140.8	140.0	141.0
Gross sown area (m hectares)	131.1	152.8	165.8	172.6	181.5
Net irrigated area	20.9	24.7	22.1	27.6	45.5
Gross irrigated area	22.6	28.0	38.2	49.8	60.5
Fertilizer-MPK (in m tonnes)	0.069	0.294	2.25	5.52	12.73
Pesticides ('000 tonnes)	2.4	8.6	24.3	45.0	79.4
Area under HYV (m hectares)	15.5	43.1	66.6		
Tractors ('000)	9	31	143	520	1550
Pumpsets ('000):					
Electricity	26	160	1620	4324	9200
Oil	83	230	1560	2810	5000
			Output		
Foodgrains (m tonnes)	50.8	82.0	108.4	129.6	176.4*
Cereals	42.4	69.3	96.6	119.0	162.1*
Pulses (m tonnes)	8.4	12.7	11.8	10.6	14.3*

| Sugarcane (m tonnes) | 57.1 | 110.0 | 126.4 | 154.2 | 241.0* |
| Oilseeds** (10^6 tons) | 5.2 | 7.0 | 9.6 | 9.4 | 18.6 |

* relates to 1990-91

** include groundnut, rapeseed and mustard, sedamum, linseed, castorseed, nigerseed, safflower, sunflower and soyabean.

Source: GOI, *Ministry of Agriculture, Indian Agriculture in Brief* (various editions).
GOI, *Economic Survey*, 1992-93.

TABLE 5

Production of selected manufactures, India 1950-51 to 1990-91

	1950-51	1960-61	1970-71	1980-81	1990-91
Coal (m tonnes)	32.3	55.2	76.3	119	225.5
Petroleum (m tonnes)	.3	.5	6.8	10.5	33.0
Electricity (b.KWH)	5.1	16.9	55.8	110.8	264.6
Finished steel (m tonnes)	1.04	2.39	4.64	6.82	13.53
Aluminium ('000 tonnes)	4.	18.50	168.80	199.00	451.00
Machine tools (Rs. mn)	3	8	430	1692	7731.00
Cotton mill machinery (Rs. mn)	–	–	303	3027	9454
Current machinery (Rs. mn)	–	6	42	336	2761
Railway wagons ('000 Nos)	–	9	11.1	13.6	25.3
Automobiles ('000 Nos)	16.5	54.8	87.9	121.1	366.3
Motorcycles, scooters etc. ('000 Nos)	–	.9	97	447.2	1842.8
Power pumps ('000 Nos)	35	105	259	431	519
Power transformers (m KVA)	0.18	1.39	8.09	19.46	36.58
Electric motors (m HP)	.73	2.72	4.06	5.86	
Nitrogen fertilizer ('000 tonnes)	9	99	830	2164	6993
Caustic soda ('000 tonnes)	12	99	371	578	992

Paper and paper board ('000 tonnes)	116	349	755	1149	2088
Cement (m tonnes)	2.7	8.	14.3	18.6	48.8
Petroleum products (m tonnes)	.2	5.7	17.1	24.1	48.
Cotton cloth (m sq.m)	4215	6738	7602	8368	15431
Mixed/blended (m sq.m)	–	–	170	1270	2371
Man-made fibre (m sq.m)	300	550	951	1350	5126
Sugar (m tonnes)	1134	3029	3740	5748	12047

Source: GOI, *Economic Survey*, 1992-93.

TABLE 6
Indicators of living standards

	1950-51 to 1954-55	1960-61 to 1964-65	1970-71 to 1974-75	1980-81 to 1984-85	1985-86 to 1989-90
Per capita availability foodgrains (gm per pay)	418.5	461.2	442.6	456	473.6
Edible oil and vanaspati (kg/year)	3.2*	3.9	4.0	6.2	6.5
Cloth cotton (metres/year)	14.4*	14.6	12.8	10.5	12.5
Man-made cloth (metres/year)	na	1.3	2.0	3.9	5.9
	1950-51	1960-61	1970-71	1980-81	1990-91
Literacy rate (per cent)					
Overall	18.3	28.3	34.4	43.6	52.2
Male	27.2	40.4	45.9	56.4	64.1
Female	8.9	15.3	22	29.7	39.3
Life expectancy of birth (years)	31.1	41.3	45.6	50.5	55.9
Registered medical practitioners (no. per 10000 population)	1.7	1.9	2.8	3.9	4.7
Hospital beds "	3.2	5.2	6.4	8.3	9.6

* Relates to 1955-56
Source: GOI, *Economic Survey, 1992-93*.

TABLE 7

Trends in employment in India 1972-73 to 1987-88
(million persons)

	1972-73	1977-78	1983-84	1987-88
Estimated no. in labour force	233	265	301	324
Estimated no. employed				
Agriculture	172	186	206	207
Non-agriculture	61	79	95	117
Employment in organized sector				
Public	na	20.7	24.1	25.9
Private	na	13.8	16.5	18.4
		6.9	7.6	7.5
Estimated usually unemployed	10.2	20.4	14.5	24

Estimated from Minhas B.S and Visaria P., "Evolving an Employment Policy for the 1990s", *Economic and Political Weekly*, 13 April, 1991.

TABLE 8
Income and expenditure of government
(Centre, State and Union Territories)

	1960-61	1970-71	1980-81	1992-93
1. Receipts	2704	7928	33394	213192
Taxes	1350	4752	19844	115331
Non-tax revenue	374	1312	4719	34958
Internal borrowing(net)	601	1482	7161	57528
External borrowing(net)	379	382	1670	5375
2.Expenditure	2586	8352	36845	220275
Non-development	836	1365	12419	91114
Defence	281	1183	3867	19620
Police	94	345	1163	6966
Interest on debt	116	716	2957	37700
Others	345	1365	4432	26828
Development	1727	4891	24426	129161
3. Overall surplus (–) or deficit (+) [(2) – (1)]	–118	424	3451	7083
4. Borrowing as % of expenditure	37	22	23	28

Centre for Monitoring Indian Economy, Basic Statistics relating to Indian Economy, August 1993.

TABLE 9

Some indicators of the importance of the public sector in the Indian economy (at current price)

	1950-51	1960-61	1970-71	1980-81	1990-91
Tax revenues as % of GDP	7.1	9.1	11.6	14.9	17.1
Share of public sector in					
Gross domestic product					
Gross domestic expenditure	na	15.9	19.8	27	33.7
Gross domestic investment	27.1	44.9	39.1	38.1	39.9
Gross domestic savings	17.2	20.6	18.5	16.2	4.5

Computed from CSO national accounts (various issues).

TABLE 10
Public Sector Plan Outlays 1961–1990

	Third plan 1961-66	Annual plans 1966-69	Fourth plan 1969-74	Fifth plan 1974-79	Annual plans 1979-80	Sixth plan 1980-85	Seventh plan 1985-90
Agriculture and allied activities	1754 (20.5)	1578 (23.8)	3674 (23.3)	8741 (22.1)	3284 (27.0)	26130 (23.9)	48100 (22.)
Industry and minerals	1726 (20.1)	1510 (22.8)	2864 (18.2)	8989 (22.8)	2383 (19.6)	15002 (13.7)	25971 (11.9)
Village and small industry	241 (2.8)	126 (1.9)	243 (1.5)	592 (1.5)	256 (2.1)	1945 (1.8)	3249 (1.5)
Power	1252 (14.6)	1212 (18.3)	2932 (18.6)	7399 (18.8)	2240 (18.4)	30751 (28.1)	61689 (28.2)
Transportation and communication	2112 (24.6)	1222 (18.4)	3080 (19.5)	6870 (17.4)	2045 (16.8)	17678 (16.2)	37974 (17.4)
Social services and others	1510 (17.4)	977 (14.8)	2986 (18.9)	6835 (17.3)	1968 (16.2)	17786 (16.3)	41747 (19.1)
Total	8595 (100.0)	6625 (100.0)	15779 (100.0)	39426 (100.0)	12176 (100.0)	109292 (100.0)	218730 (100.0)

Note: Figures in brackets relate to share of each sector in total outlay.
Source: Centre for Monitoring Indian Economy, Basic Statistics relating to Indian Economy, 1993.

Notes

NOTES TO CHAPTER 1

1. The paper, published in 1993 is titled "Economic Reforms: Two Years after and the Task Ahead". Our discussion of Structural Reforms on the following pages is based on this paper.

NOTES TO CHAPTER 2

1. GOI, (1952). See especially chapters 1 and 2. The quotes on pp. 14–16 are all from this document.
2. See especially the Bombay Plan. Thakurdas *et al.* (1944).
3. The architect of this strategy was Prof. P.C. Mahalonobis, who founded the Indian Statistical Insitute at Calcutta, served as Honorary Statistical Advisor to the Government of India and later as Member of the Planning Commission.
4. The first systematic consideration of these aspects is to be found in the Reports of the Committee on Distribution of Women and Levels of Living (1964 and 1969) appointed by the Government of India and in Hazari 1966.

   The National Sample Survey has collected regularly, since the early 1950s, massive amounts of information on the assets, consumption, employment, literacy and several other related aspects bearing on the living standards of the people. These data tell us a great deal about the inequality in wealth and consumption between different segments of the population, as well as access to basic needs. This has stimulated a great deal of work on the incidence of poverty, characteristics of the poor, and the determinants of poverty. See Bardhan and Srinivasan, 1974 and 1989.

5. This view was presented in a paper entitled "Notes on Perspectives of Development in India: 1960-61 to 1975-76, Implications of Planning for a Minimum Level of Living" GOI, Planning Commision, 1964.

6. These include the Committee on Import and Export Policies (1978) headed by P.C. Alexander; Committee on Controls and Subsidies headed by Vadilal Dagli; Committee on Reform of Economic Administration headed by L.K. Jha, and a report on public sector reform prepared by A. Sengupta.

NOTES TO CHAPTER 3

1. The estimates for 1959 are from Hazari's book *Structure of the Corporate Private Sector* (1966). For 1989-90 the CMIE gives the names of the top 20 business houses and estimates their total assets at Rs 41,500 crores, compared to the total assets of selected 2330 private corporations estimated at Rs 170,366 crores (CMIE 1993)

2. The growth of real output during the first half of the twentieth century was barely two per cent a year in the aggregate and half a percent or less a year in per capita terms. Heston, 1983.

3. These figures are taken from the World Bank's *World Development Report 1990*.

4. Suryanarayana (1986) reports that inequality in the distribution of consumption in rural India (and most states) does not show any sustained, or significant trend—cited in Mahendra Dev *et al*. 1992.

5. This is from a report by Acharya and others on 'Aspects of Black Economy in India' prepared for the National Institute of Public Finance and Policy in 1985. The estimate of this report implies an increase in the ratio of black income to official GDP between 1975 and 1980.

6. These estimates are from the report of an expert committee on poverty estimates appointed by the Planning Commission GOI, PC 1993.

7. These estimates are from Mundle and Rao 1991.
8. Computed from data published by the Bureau of Public Enterprises (for public undertakings) and by the Reserve Bank (for corporate sector).

NOTES TO CHAPTER 4

1. The second plan strategy was criticised by Vakil and Brahmananda (1956) for ignoring the need and scope for utilizing surplus labour for investment and increasing output of mass consumption goods, and by Shenoy on the ground that it was physically and financially unviable, would aggravate inflation, add to social tensions and undermine orderly progress. In the context of the third plan, criticisms emphasised over-rating political and financial feasibility, excessive optimum on balance of payments, neglect of employment aspects and the lack of a policy frame. (Little 1962, Gadgil 1967, Lewis 1968). The emphasis on poverty alleviation and basic needs started with the PPD paper on minimum living standards and was articulated further in Dandekar and Rath 1971, Minhas 1974. The criticisms of overall strategy focussing on the deleterious effects of import substitution, controls and licensing have been discussed at length by Bhagwati and Desai 1970, Bhagwati and Srinivasan 1975 and recently by Ahluwalia 1985.
2. An elaboration of this viewpoint is contained in Vaidyanathan 1993.
3. The inequality of access to elementary education, health care and the basic amenities is brought out by the NSS survey on social consumption. See Sarvekshana, Jan–Mar 1991.

    For a useful survey of the experience of poverty alleviation schemes see Mahendra Dev et al. 1993, which also gives references to a number of evaluation studies.
4. For a critical review of the planning process, see Paranjape 1964, Hanson 1970, and Reports of the Administrative Reforms Commission.
5. The Sarkaria Commission report reviewed Centre-State relations comprehensively and made a number of important recommendations for reform. See also Krishnaswamy et al. 1992.
6. For a discussion of the political economy of Indian development

from various perspectives, see Frankel 1979, Rudolph and Rudolph 1987, Raj 1971, Bardhan 1984, Kohli 1987.

7. This view is advocated by Bardhan 1985. For other views, see Raj 1971 and Rudolph and Rudolph 1987.

NOTES TO CHAPTER 5

1. For a recent assessment of the East Asia experience, see (World Bank 1993) *The East Asian Miracle: Economic Growth and Public Policy*, Oxford University Press.

2. A forceful statement of this is contained in Gulati and Sharma 1991, Pursell and Gulati 1993.

References

Ahluwalia, Isher J. (1985), "Industrial Growth in India: Stagnation since the Mid-Sixties", Oxford University Press, New Delhi, in Bardhan *et al.* (eds.).

Bardhan, P.K. (1984), *The Political Economy of Development in India*, Oxford University Press, New Delhi.

Bhagwati, J.N. and P. Desai (1970), *Planning for Industrialisation: India's Trade and Industrialist Politics, 1950–66*, Oxford University Press, New Delhi.

Bhagwati, J.N. and T.N. Srinivasan (1975), *Foreign Trade Regimes and Economic Development: India*, National Bureau of Economic Research, New Delhi.

Centre for Monitoring of Indian Economy (1993), *Basic Statistics Relating to Indian Economy*, Vol. 1.

Dandekar, V.M. and N. Rath (1971), *Poverty in India*, Indian School of Political Economy, Lonavala.

Frankel, Francine R. (1978), *India's Political Economy 1947–1977: The Gradual Revolution*, Princeton.

Gadgil, D.R. (1967), "Planning Without a Policy Frame", *Economic and Political Weekly*, Annual Number.

GOI Planning Commission (1952), *The First Five Year Plan*, New Delhi.

GOI Planning Commission (1964), *Report of the Committee on*

Distribution of Incomes and Level of Living, Part I: *Distribution of Income and Wealth and Concentration of Economic Power,* New Delhi.

GOI Planning Commission (1969), *Report of the Committee on Distribution of Incomes and Levels of Living,* Part II: *Changes in Level of Living,* New Delhi.

GOI Planning Commission (1993), *Reports of the Expert Group on Estimate of the Proportion and Number of Poor,* New Delhi.

Gulati, Ashok and P.K. Sharma (1991), "Government Intervention in Agricultural Markets: Nature, Import and Implications", *Journal of Indian School of Political Economy,* April-June.

Hanson, A.H. (1966), *The Process of Planning: A Study of India's Five Year Plan 1950–1964,* Oxford Univeristy Press, New Delhi.

Hazari, R.K. (1966), *Structure of the Corporate Private Sector: A Study of Concentration, Ownership and Control,* Bombay.

Heston, A. (1983), "National Income" in D. Kumar (ed.), *Cambridge Economic History of India,* Vol. 2: 1957–c. 1970, Cambridge University Press, Cambridge.

Kohli, Atul (1987), *State and Poverty in India: Politics of Reform.*

Krishnaswamy, K.S., I.S. Gulati and A. Vaidyanathan (1992), "Economic Aspects of Federalism in India", in Mukkarji, Nirmal and B.Arora (eds.), *Federalism in India: Origins and Development,* Vikas, New Delhi.

Lewis, John P. (1963), *Quiet Crisis in India,* Washington.

Little, I.M.D. (1962), *A Critical Examination of India's Third Five Year Plan,* Oxford Economic Papers.

Mahendra Dev, S. (1993), *Development and Change: Essays in Honour of K.N. Raj,* Oxford University Press, New Delhi.

Minhas, B.S. (1974), *Planning and the Poor,* S. Chand, New Delhi.

Mundle, Sudipto and Govinda Rao (1991), "Volume and Composition of Government Subsidies 1987–88", *Economic and Political Weekly,* May 4.

National Institute of Public Finance and Policy (1985), "Aspects of the Black Economy of India: Draft Report", New Delhi (mimeo).

Parike, K.S. and M.H. Suryanarayana (1993), *Rural Poverty in India:*

114

Issues and Policies, Indira Gandhi Institute of Development Research, Bombay.

Paranjape, H.K. (1964), *Planning Commission: A Descriptive Account*, Indian Institute of Public Administration, New Delhi.

Pursell, Garry and Ashok Gulati (1993), *Liberalising Indian Agriculture: An Agenda for Reform*, World Bank Working Paper Series No. 1172 (mimeo).

Raj, K.N. (1971), "The Class Structure in India and Some of its Implications for Economic Policy and Planning" (mimeo).

Rudolph, Lloyd and Susanne Rudolph (1987), *In Pursuit of Lakshmi: The Political Economy of the Indian State*, Orient Longman, Bombay.

Suryanarayana, M.A. (1986), "The Problem of Distribution in India's Development", unpublished Ph.D. thesis, Indian Statistical Institute.

Thakurdas, Purushotamdas *et al.* (1964), *Plan for Economic Development of India*.

Vakil, C.N. and P.R. Brahmananda (1956), *Planning for a Shortage Economy*, Bombay.